GU00319458

Empsons' War

Empsons' War

A collection of letters

C. C. Empson

The Pentland Press
Edinburgh – Cambridge – Durham – USA

First published in 1995 by
The Pentland Press Ltd
1 Hutton Close
South Church
Bishop Auckland
Durham

British Library
Cataloguing in Publication Data.
A catalogue record for this book
is available from the British Library.

ISBN 1-85821-259-6

Typeset by Carnegie Publishing, 18 Maynard St., Preston.
Printed and bound by Antony Rowe Ltd., Chippenham.

For

Arthur, Jack and Charles

Contents

Introduction

The protagonists in this war were very young. Jack, the eldest, was only 23 when he took his last flight; Charles, the youngest, was the same age when he described the entry of the High Commissioner into Baghdad.

Perhaps a short introduction is due to explain some of the references and describe the background. There's no necessity to read it. My notes will follow the same order as the list of contents, from Ireland before the war to Iraq a few years later. I hope this will not detract from the spontaneity and spirit of the letters.

ARTHUR IN IRELAND

In the late nineteenth century Mr Gladstone had crucified the Liberal party with his Home Rule Bills. A new land act, the Irish Land Purchase Act, had been passed in 1903, by which tenants could buy their farms aided with government funds. By 1914 two thirds of arable land in Ireland had changed hands and the absentee landlord had all but disappeared. The Liberal Government of 1905 was again pledged to Home Rule. In 1912 Redmond, leader of the Nationalists, pressed for Home Rule and the Government introduced the Third Home Rule Bill, but it was rejected by the House of Lords. The Protestants in Ulster, under Sir Edward Carson, prepared to defy the terms of the Bill and to build up a private army, the Ulster Volunteers. Meanwhile the Nationalists started to form the National Volunteers.

There was a crisis when British cavalry officers stationed at the Curragh declared that they would take no part in the coercion of Ulster, but the House of Lords continued to oppose the Home Rule Bill. Asquith was hesitant, so all was uncertainty and there was danger of civil war in Ireland, but the European crisis intervened. By the time Arthur wrote his last letter from Ireland, the Archduke Ferdinand had been assassinated at Sarajevo (28th June 1914), Austria had mobilized against Serbia and Germany had declared war on both Russia and France. Mobilization means war – Schlieffen's principle was fulfilled and it only needed the violation of Belgian territory for Britain to declare war on Germany (4th August 1914).

I

There was an uneasy peace in Ireland until the 1916 Easter Rebellion by which time Arthur was dug in on the Western Front. Evidently he made the common mistake of thinking the war would soon be over – only Lord Kitchener predicted correctly that it would last at least three years. In the event Arthur never reached Potsdam but he had enough adventure to make up for it.

JACK AND THE ROYAL FLYING CORPS

Jack's letter from school was probably written in 1910. The Emperor William II visited England twice before the outbreak of war, for the funeral of his cousin Edward VII in 1910 and again for the unveiling of his grandmother's Memorial in front of Buckingham Palace the following year. Later, when relations between Britain and Germany had deteriorated, included in George V's heavy correspondence was discussion of the alleged pro-German utterances of the Headmaster of Eton.

The letter from Lichfield was written during the course of the coal strike of 26 February to 11 April, 1912. It cost the country 30 million working days. The miners were demanding a minimum wage of 5s a day for men and 2s a day for boys. The result was the Minimum Wages Bill which was introduced on March 19th and received the Royal Assent on 29 March, indicating the alarm shown by politicians and citizens alike at the supposed threat from the demands of organized labour. The celebrations at Yokefleet would also have been in 1912, before Jack became a graduate of the central Flying School.

The RFC was founded in 1912 by Royal Warrant. Number Two Squadron had carried out a manoeuvre to prove its self-sufficiency by moving from Farnborough to Montrose by road, rail and air. The CO was Major Charles James Burke, seconded from the Royal Irish Regiment. He saw the need to bring the discipline of war to aviation and the Squadron had crossed the Irish Sea to take part in the Irish Command Manoeuvres. The purpose of the return flight to Farnborough, according to the Yorkshire Post, was 'not so much a test of the flying machine but as a criterion of the abilities of the motor transport section to keep pace with them. After leaving York, which will probably be used as a permanent aeroplane depot, the intervening stopping places were to be Lincoln, Northampton and Oxford.' Jack had already been to York to settle advance details of this early essay in aeronautical logistics. His mother wrote to her sister (whose twin sons both became Air Marshals) on 6 May: 'We found Jack at Driffield Terrace. He had come over to arrange landing grounds for the Montrose Flying Corps. He says the twelve aeroplanes and all their sheds and paraphernalia will arrive on Knavesmire on May

15 (Friday) and stay till Monday morning, on their way to Salisbury Plain. Why don't you motor to York on the Saturday and see them all?' But only three of the twelve aircraft from the squadron ever arrived in York.

CHARLES AT OFFICER CADET SCHOOL

The barracks at Ordnance Hill, St Johns Wood, are still used by the King's Troop, Royal Horse Artillery, whence they proceed through Marble Arch to fire ceremonial salutes in Hyde Park.

Horatio Bottomley was the most successful of the recruiting orators in the days of Kitchener and, before conscription was introduced (January 1916), his fees for speaking ranged from less than £100 for simple patriotism to over £200 for oratory stirring the blood to religious fervour. He made £78,000 for himself, spent largely on racehorses, women and champagne; so he would make an ideal subject for satire in a play, and a suitable plaintiff in an unsuccessful action for libel.

The Great War marked great advances in political rights for women. Mrs Pankhurst has already been mentioned in a letter from Ireland; the violent era of the suffragette campaign culminated in 1913 with the death of Emily Davison under the hooves of the King's horse at the Derby. As Minister of Munitions Lloyd George gave women the 'right to work' in the shell factories, and hundreds of thousands proved their worth, also as typists and office clerks. Voluntary Aid Detachment provided feminine support closer to the fighting line. Ten years after the war the vote was finally extended to all women over the age of twenty-one.

Charles was later to know two extraordinary manifestations of emancipated womanhood – Gertrude Bell, director of Antiquities at the Iraq Museum, which she founded in Baghdad, and who became de facto political adviser to the Government by the weight of her experience; and later Freya Stark, explorer and writer, who startled the expatriates of the city by taking up residence in the red light district.

ARTHUR AT THE FRONT

The field censors did their job so effectively that it is difficult to deduce where Arthur was much of the time or the sequence of events described, as so many of the letters are undated. An attempt has been made to put them in a logical order, but their anecdotal nature means that little is lost by not knowing when and where things happened. It seems that he was on the Front almost throughout hostilities, was at the Royal Herbert Military Hospital in Shooters Hill Road at least once, and was reported killed.

The middle period of the war saw each side trying to destroy the other's man-power by sheer weight of gunfire, followed by infantry assault. The French have a phrase for it: *L'artillerie conquért, l'infanterie occupe.* But the assaults seldom led to significant gains because the trench system was almost impregnable.

The stalemate on the ground was broken in 1917; as far as the letters are concerned on 14 July . . . a climactic moment when Arthur describes the effect upon him of the mining, not only because he was permanently deafened, but because the Mines at Messines on 7 June, heard according to A. J. P. Taylor by Lloyd George in Downing Street (rather than Walton Heath) marked a turning point in the war. Only a few hundred yards had been gained: trench warfare was both futile and murderous. So frustrating to soldiers trained to open warfare, the pattern was broken soon after by the opening of the 3rd Battle of Ypres or Passchendaele. The failure of Ludendorf's great offensive in 1918 led to talk of peace.

There is a note of disillusion in the tone of the final letters, reflecting the general feeling in the country. There were reasons for this. Lloyd George precipitated an early election for suspect political reasons, and there were fears that the troops might be disenfranchised if the election was too hasty. The order of demobilization seemed unfair, especially to those who had been at the front from the start. There was a feeling that the country was not offering a home-coming fit for heroes. Organized labour flexed its muscles again and there was social unrest early in 1919. In 1919–20 there were two thousand strikes great and small. Luton Town Hall was burnt down and there were riots in Glasgow and Belfast.

As soon as victory was assured Lloyd George wanted immediate elections as the present Parliament had exceeded its statutory term of life, and he hoped to prolong the Coalition government but he needed Unionist support. He entered into a contract with Bonar Law under which all candidates who were classed as loyal to the Coalition were to receive a badge or certificate in the form of a letter of recommendation jointly signed by the two politicians. So the election of December 1918 became known as the Coupon Election, and was duly won by the Coalition while Mr Asquith, standing as Independent Liberal, was defeated at East Fife. Thus the election gave Lloyd George and his government an overwhelming mandate to direct their policy of peace and reconstruction after the war.

Both Britain and Germany had long standing interests in Turkish Meso-potamia. The Germans were pursuing the *Drang nach Osten* policy with their ambitious project for the Berlin–Baghdad railway; they were also active in archaeology and in military training. The British were most involved in navigation on the Tigris and Euphrates, and in irrigation projects on the desert fringe supervised by Sir William Willcocks. The origin of river steamer traffic on the Tigris can be traced back many years, the earliest ventures being those of the firm of Stephen Lynch & Co. The Euphrates and Tigris Steam Navigation Company was formed and incorporated in England in 1861, a limited number of steam boats being operated under the authority of an Imperial Firman, granted by the Sultan of Turkey.

However, when Turkey joined the Central Powers in 1914, Britain woke up to the fact that she would have to take action to protect the wells and pipe lines of the Anglo-Iranian Oil Company. A Turkish attack on the Suez Canal was repulsed and in November 1914 Britain retaliated by occupying Basrah. The German defeat of Serbia emphasized the vulnerability of British interests in the Middle East. The military side-shows in Mesopotamia and Palestine, not only to regain prestige after the withdrawal from Gallipoli but to protect both the Persian Gulf and the Suez Canal, became an important part of British strategy. These two operations were respectively entrusted to the Mesopo-tamian and Egyptian Expeditionary Forces, of which the first was despatched by the Indian and the second by the Home Government. For the first two years of the war the India Office was responsible in Whitehall both for policy and for control of military operations in Mesopotamia. After the capture of Kut al Amara the War Office took over the military operations but political responsibility remained in the hands of the India Office. The 117th Mahrattas, sent by the G.H.Q. Simla as part of Force D, distinguished itself in these campaigns.

An over-hasty advance up the river system had turned to disaster in December 1915 when General Townsend was surrounded at Kut al Amara and forced to surrender with 9,000 men.

Prestige had to be restored to the extent that by the end there were 600,000 British and Indian troops in the Middle East theatre of war. On March 11th 1917 General Maude captured Baghdad; on 9th December General Allenby received the surrender of Jerusalem, entering on foot two days later.

Charles had to make the best of his posting to Peshawar. This was a traditional role for the British Army. Ever since the Afghan War, 1839–42, and the Crimean War, 1854–56, there seemed to be a necessity to defend

5

imperial interests on the North-West Frontier from possible Russian incursion, and to keep control of the indigenous tribes on the Afghan Border. However, Russia was an ally until the 1917 Revolution took her out of the war, so Charles's determination to fight a Russian was misplaced and by the time he arrived in Baghdad there was no necessity to kill a Turk.

ARTHUR IN TURKEY

The Germans, with their Mitteleuropa policy, promoted by Falkenhayn had opened the road to Constantinople with the conquest of Serbia and had pursued their influence eastward with the advance of the Berlin–Baghdad railway. In April 1915 Constantinople had been promised to Russia, Syria to the French, while British agents, notably Sir Ronald Storrs (see his memoirs *Orientations*) were soon to be tempting the Arabs to revolt against Turkish rule with promises and gold. So there were likely to be complications when peace eventually came. On 30 October Turkey signed an armistice of surrender; the British navy steamed through the Dardanelles and Constantinople passed into allied control.

In 1920 by the Treaty of Sèvres (all part of the Versailles settlement) Turkey was to keep Constantinople, Thrace and Asia Minor, but Smyrna was to be under Greek control. It was this provision that caused the situation when Arthur was stationed there in 1920.

Mustapha Kemal, later known as Ataturk, had already distinguished himself by forcing the British withdrawal from Gallipoli. In 1920 Allied troops turned the Kemalists out of Constantinople but his adherents, the Nationalists, continued to harry the Greeks round Smyrna and to defy the terms of the Treaty of Sèvres. So the allies were obliged to garrison the neutral 12 mile deep 'Zone of the Straits' at Charnak and Istanbul with a peace-keeping force between Turk and Greek. Arthur's letters illustrate the delicate nature of this role.

Eventually the Nationalists drove the Greeks from Smyrna, but the decisive factor in the withdrawal of Greek interests was probably the death of Alexander, King of the Hellenes, and the defeat of Venizelos in the Greek elections. Ataturk was then able to negotiate a new treaty at Lausanne in 1923 which established the modern Turkish state.

CHARLES IN THE HIGH COMMISSIONERS OFFICE

A British army under Allenby reached Damascus on 1 October 1918, while another was moving up the Euphrates to the oil wells of Mosul. This was eighteen months after the capture of Baghdad. The policy in both capitals was ostensibly the same. The British had come to Baghdad as to Damascus 'not as conquerors but as liberators'. They were bound by the promise given to Sherif Hussein in 1916 that they would 'recognize and support the independence of the Arabs' and it was their object in the ancient capitals of the Abbasid and Ommeyyad alike to re-establish Arab rule.

Already it was acknowledged that direct British administration was at variance with Arab ideals, although the area remained under British administration through the duration of the war. However, in January 1918, President Wilson enunciated his Fourteen Points, of which the twelfth laid down that the nationalities other than Turkish which were then under Turkish rule should be assured security of life and an absolute opportunity for autonomy. Then Article 22 of the Covenant of the League of Nations, approved on 28th April 1919, and included in negotiations which led to the Treaty of Versailles on 28th June, enshrined a new principle to be known as the mandatory system by which territories formerly in the Turkish Empire should be put under the tutelage of the allied powers, in this case France and Britain. Britain similarly became the mandatory power in Palestine. There was considerable muddle, partly because of the ambiguous promise to the Arabs, and partly because, quite unforeseen, the treaty with Turkey took six years to finalize. For Palestine there was the added complication of the Balfour Declaration. In the summer of 1920 there was a serious Arab rebellion in Mesopotamia, put down at considerable trouble and cost; the Arabs were losing faith in their infidel rulers. So there was a persistent demand from the British public at home that the Mesopotamian question should be settled.

First in October 1920 Sir Percy Cox, who had been Political Officer in Baghdad during the war and Minister in Teheran, was appointed High Commissioner. Then, in March 1921, Mr Churchill who had recently organized a special Middle Eastern Department in the Colonial Office to deal with Arab affairs, summoned a conference at Cairo, known as the Middle East Conference, to review the whole situation. This decided the future of Iraq.

A declared objective for Churchill was to reduce imperial expenditure in the Middle East: the length of Charles's cigar was not entirely irrelevant. The way to achieve this, consistent with the mandate, was to set the relations between Britain and Iraq upon a treaty footing. Churchill was advised that Faisal was the man with whom the treaty should be made. The future king was informed that there would be no objection to his visiting Iraq and offering himself as candidate for the throne on the understanding that if he were crowned King he would, by treaty, enable Britain to fulfil her mandatory responsibilities. Faisal landed at Basrah in June, was crowned in August and

7

formed the first Council of Ministers in September 1921. The High Commissioner ceased in effect to have executive authority, becoming adviser to the King and his ministers. The question then arose whether British officials were servants of His Majesty's Government or of the Iraqi Government. As it happened King Faisal lived on the left bank of the Tigris and Sir Percy Cox on the right, so it became practice to refer to relations between the two banks of the river and this was the system that applied for the next ten years.

Faisal's brother, Abdullah, was offered the principality of Trans-Jordan; his father, Sherif Hussein, the southerly kingdom of Hejaz. The ascendancy of the Hashemite dynasty seemed assured. Sir Herbert Samuel became first High Commissioner in Palestine. But, although the conference took place at Cairo, the problem of Egypt was the most persistent. As Charles was there throughout the Second World War in Lord Killearn's Embassy and had a prolonged experience of that 'ripping place', it seems only right to continue the story of Anglo-Egyptian relations. The Great War broke the enchantment of absolute British rule which had lasted since 1882 when Mr Gladstone, of all people, ordered the occupation leading to the defeat of Arabi Pasha by General Wolseley at Tel-el-Kebir.

A wartime declaration established Egypt as a British protectorate; her strategic importance was obviously immense, but nationalism grew stronger throughout the war, and by 1919 Cairo was a revolutionary city, partly because the British had deported the nationalist leader, Sa-ad Zaghlul Pasha, to Malta. Allenby allowed him to return, saving the situation temporarily, because his party, the Wafd, did not advocate violence hoping to negotiate the British out of Egypt. In July 1921 an Egyptian delegation under the Premier, Adly Pasha, visited London to negotiate a permanent settlement, but it failed and Zaghlul was exiled a second time. At last in February 1922 the British Government, to prevent a deteriorating situation, announced the termination of the Protectorate and recognized Egypt as an independent sovereign state. The Khediv Fuad became King and was succeeded by his son, Farouk.

Charles was strangely dismissive of Lawrence 'the Arab impersonator'. Perhaps it was already fashionable for the young to debunk national heroes; since then Lawrence's role in the war against Turkey has been under scrutiny and questioned. However, by 1933, Charles owned a copy of *The Independent Arab* by Sir Hubert Young, who participated in Lawrence's exploits and vividly describes their association from their first meeting at Carcemish where a British expedition was excavating the old Hittite capital and a 'quiet little man of the name of Lawrence who was for some reason living there alone' showed them round the digs because Woolley was away; his emergence as an inspiring leader; the capture of Akaba; the Deraa raid and the harassing of the

8

Hejaz railway; the Imperial Camel Corps and the Sherifian army; and the final race for Damascus. Maybe Charles was converted, but in 1920 he seemed to be sceptical of archaeology and had probably been a soldier recently enough to be annoyed at Lawrence's undisguised contempt for the regular soldierman.

The Great War proved a strong incentive to the development of flying. The Royal Flying Corps in 1914 had about three hundred aircraft. The Royal Air Force, established as an independent service in April 1918, under Sir Hugh Trenchard, had over twenty thousand by the end of the War. A fortnightly mail service was introduced between Cairo and Baghdad. The fly-past over Baghdad was more than ceremonial; air support became important for containment of the constant insurrections by the Kurds from their mountain homes. Charles later had a favourite story that a propaganda mission with a megaphone over the mountains was apparently frustrated because the bringer of peace was being violently air-sick; but all was well because the Kurds, terrified by the noises reverberating about them, immediately surrendered. He also compared the Arch of Ctesiphon unfavourably with Howden airfield; this might seem a strange judgement, until one remembers that Howden was base for the Naval Airship Station where there were likely to be hangars at least the height of the Arch of Ctesiphon.

Charles remained in Iraq until 1934 by which time it was a sovereign country. His next post was Haifa in Palestine where he remained a committed Arabist. The Iraq he knew ceased violently many years later with the murder of Faisal II in 1958, and the end of the Hashemite dynasty there. Now Saddam Hussein reigns.

THE FAMILY

The Empsons are of yeoman stock (see Arthur's reference) from the Isle of Axholme and the Goole Marshlands area. There was a Royalist brother, George, who is buried in Hook Church near Goole, and a Parliamentarian brother, Jonathan, whose present whereabouts are unknown, though perhaps in a field behind Goole Hall where there is a family burial ground. They set themselves up as gentlemen about this time but their coat of arms was respited for proof at the 1662 visitation and they remained in disgrace until Arthur put the matter right with a consideration to the College of Arms some years ago.

Their father died in March 1916; most of the letters are therefore addressed to their mother who moved to York after her husband's death. Arthur did not go to India but joined the Territorials in Hull to be near the property which was unexpectedly his, and finally left the army to live at Yokefleet where he died in 1973.

9

There are references to warp or warping. This is a local term for river silt deposited by high tides on the Ouse and Humber estuary. Natural warping is how nature intended it before the river banks were raised, and the whole area was a broad flood plain. Artificial warp is the result of high tides being deliberately channelled onto the land over a period of two years or so in order to increase the fertility of the soil. The Empsons have always had a proper respect for mud. Arthur warped sixty acres at Blacktoft in 1950/51 for the hell of it and to honour a family tradition going back 150 years, but it would be uneconomic today owing to the tremendous earth works required. He was probably the last practitioner. But you get the atmosphere of this strangely remote-seeming place in a poem called Flighting for Duck by the youngest brother, occasionally referred to in the letters, who became William Empson, poet and critic. And maybe this was evocative too for Charles when he was at Basrah. Apart from the heat and the date palms, the estuary landscape must have made him feel at home; and he probably admired the earthen Shaiba Bund constructed by the British to protect the city from the Euphrates' floods. For him too, the Postscript somehow seems appropriate, though people round Yokefleet and Blacktoft would not have invested a wood-pigeon with the grand Latin name used by the Natural History Museum. They would have called it a stoggie.

Arthur

Ireland

Arthur
Ireland

Royal Field Artillery, Waterford

My dear Father

I arrived here all right on Sunday morning at 7 o'clock after a perfectly beastly crossing – I wasn't actually ill though. I did not pay anything for extra luggage north of London but I had to stump up 15/- at Paddington.

The mess consists at present of Peck and myself. It's a blessing I was not rude to him in my letters. The two other subalterns are on leave and the captain and major are both married. Messing here is naturally very expensive as there are only four of us altogether. Last month the catering was 5/6 a day (it was 4/- at Bordon) a piece apart from subscriptions or extras – which is a penny a day less than the pay. We are trying to economise by living on ham and cold beef until the others return.

Thanks very much for your valuable present. I found it on my arrival on Sunday. There is a lot of hunting to be got which is very near and good, and a few snipe here and there.

The battery left all its horses in England when it came over here in October and took on another lot which had been managed by some contractors who must have made a very good thing out of it, as there was very little left but skin and bones. So most of them are only allowed to be walked about while they are being fattened up, and none are huntable which is a blow! I have just had a hard day on my ten toes with some beagles owned by the Captain Staveley with whom I had such a long correspondence. He is an excellent man and I can't understand why he wouldn't give me the leave I asked for. The Major is also very restful after old Coats at Bordon.

Your affect son,
Arthur

P.S.   I don't want to rub it in, but this most certainly not a poor man's station.

13

Royal Field Artillery, Fermoy

My dear Father

There has been great excitement here about the Ulster business; but we were not mobilised or anything of that sort. I always thought that what Asquith now says was true – that is, that Sir A. Paget suddenly thought that a few more troops in Ulster would do no harm. I can't see what there is to fight about yet, so I did not spend five pounds on a revolver. But I trust all this will have the effect of stopping the Home Rule Bill. About 2 out of 3 officers in the garrison say they will resign rather than serve against Ulster, but I don't know whether they will or not. It would be rather poor fun, unless the Tories reinstate us all. I think we are in quite a good position here, as they will probably need us in the South. But when we go to Kildare we shall be in the middle of it all, just when the Bill has been passed.

I hope you are quite well again now and able to walk without impediment.

Your affectionate son
Arthur

P.S. The Cavalry Brigade apparently agreed to do 'police work' if called upon. But who is to tell where that ends and genuine fighting begins?

*　*　*

My dear Mother

A Tommy in the other barracks has caught foot and mouth disease from a dog. I believe it is only very rarely that a human being catches it, but it is an unpleasing complaint when it does happen.

I don't believe the Government will do much coercing of Ulster; they daren't even squash Mrs. Pankhurst. The gentry hereabouts – who are all Unionists – hate most of all the idea of the exclusion of Ulster, which will leave them absolutely in the lurch and must mean heavier taxation for the rest of Ireland. And for that reason I think Home Rule without Ulster can't last long. Everybody with land of their own, that is all the small farmers, dread it now because it will put them in the power of the landless man.

I'm growing out of all my clothes, including uniform which is an unforeseen calamity. We are having beastly weather here now, raining and blowing nearly all day. I hope you are better off.

Your loving son, Arthur

My dear Mother

I've just come back from a 'section march'. One section in the battery was made up to War Strength and then its commander (one 2nd Lt Swinton) has to take it for a trek in the country for two nights. On the second or third day the Major came out and said 'You're being attacked by cavalry from behind that wood' etc. etc.

We bivouacked in a field each night and had to make our own arrangements for hiring a field, buying forage, meat, bread etc. out of a government grant of £10 as we went along. I had to do all the bargaining and managed the officers' food – there was a Terr'ier subaltern attached. The first thing to do on arriving at the camping ground is to find the farmer, and produce a bottle of whisky and a glass – a little water perhaps, in case of emergency – and not to mention 'business' until you've been promoted to Major, and then only in an off-hand way. They take a pride in being close when they're out for a deal, but 'between friends' they couldn't be more generous. We didn't spend nearly all our money and more than enough of everything. It was glorious weather the whole time and altogether I enjoyed it.

I'm trying to find the best stream for Father with the least uncomfortable pub close to it. It's very hard to get any reliable information out of Irishmen; one generally gets a 'pleasant answer' but is not much wiser at the end of it.

I'm glad to hear that the foal is a nice one.

Your loving son
Arthur

*   *   *

My dear Mother

I went to the Leicester Regiment Sergeants' Dance last night. The etiquette was strange and very strict. For instance you 'sat out' before the dance instead of after. There were only two waltzes all the evening, the remainder being valetas, quadrilles etc. It was funny to see them all solemnly mincing about, dancing and retiring etc.

I've bought a horse; it has only one eye but otherwise I think it's the best horse I've ever ridden. The only effect of the blind eye was to reduce its price. I had some difficulty in getting it 'on the strength' as a charger and so drawing forage for it; but with my old Major it's all a question of the time of day. If

One of Arthur's horses at Fermoy

anyone were to ask him for any favour before lunch (he doesn't eat breakfast) he probably wouldn't get an answer at all; for anything not very important, just after dinner will do, when he is very cheery; but if you want anything out of the ordinary you have to wait till 11–12 or even 12.30 – it just depends what it is. After twelve o'clock, if one succeeds in getting a word in at all, he would agree to anything.

I hope Molly is none the worse for her fall.

The Dook of Devonshire and lots of little Ds come out with the United Hunt. He is very unpopular because he proposed the rejection of the Home Rule Bill, and last Wednesday groups of mountainy men collected with a view to scragging the old 'blowhard' if he got separated from the rest of the field; as a matter of fact, the day was blank till late on in the afternoon so all was well.

> Your loving son
> Arthur

*   *   *

> R.A. Mess   Coolmoney Camp, Co. Wicklow.

My dear Father

We arrived here yesterday after rather an amusing march. It rained for two days which were beastly but the other three were very fine and not too hot. We hit very comfy hotels at the various towns where we stayed. The men and horses were billeted – compulsorily of course – on the inhabitants, and we had to go round to see that they were being properly treated. Some of them were very hospitable and did them very well; others tried to do us out of the corn and put them 4 or 5 in one bed, until the Major sent for the Constabulary which had an instantaneous effect. They would try to haggle over the government rate of payment which was certainly very small. One gentleman, who was the local Secretary of the Gaelic League or something of the sort, apparently looked upon it as his duty as a 'patriot' to do as little as he could.

I'm sorry you can't come to Fermoy but I hope you will get here. The station is Dunlavin, ten miles from here. It is very pretty and just the place for the purpose but the accommodation is not anything to shout about.

It's very bad luck on Mab to get kicked after distinguishing herself so.

> Your affectionate son
> Arthur

*   *   *

Sunday 8th June R.A. Mess, Coolmoney Camp, Co. Wicklow.

My dear Mother

We are having beautiful weather here today although it pelted all last night. There are two F.A. Brigades here (6 batteries all together). The glen is a semi-circle about 4 miles across each way with very high hills all round it. On the side of these are disappearing targets made to represent Infantry, batteries in action etc. and the game is for these to pop up suddenly from 1 to 4 miles away while we are going along the road. One battery performs at a time while the remainder of the Officers stand around and jeer, while the General and his staff make rude remarks and also give marks. The point is to get as many effective shells onto the target in a given time, after getting into action in the best way and place possible. The Major's reputation depends a great deal on how we come out, and as ours depends entirely on him, we are very much on our good behaviour.

Jack ought to win the *Daily Mail*'s £5000; they should make him a Commander-in-Chief in the Flying Corps.

>   Your loving son
>   Arthur

*   *   *

R.A. Mess. Coolmoney Camp, Wicklow.

My dear Father

It continues to pelt with rain here and it's impossible to see well enough to fire today. Sir Arthur Paget (A.P.) came down yesterday to see the firing. He went with the ranging party near the target which was a lot of little dummies popping up at intervals, supposed to represent cavalry advancing towards the battery. In order to make the dummies clearer the staff had turned them sideways so that you could see the horses' heads, which of course made them appear to be going from left to right. The battery commander thought he'd find the range by experiment to a point well in front of them, so as to be ready for them when they arrived. The net result was that shells were bursting round the gallant Commander-in-Chief. Immediately whistles began to blow and our old Brigadier started waving his stick and shouting 'Stop! Can't any Pygmalioned fool in the battery see the target etc. etc.' But apparently no harm was done as the old man was most genial when he emerged with the ranging party.

18

Royal Field Artillery, Fermoy.

My dear Mother

I rejoice to hear that Toby is restored to the bosom (is that the way to spell it?) of his family. Mrs. Toby was only a grass widow for 10 days after all. I hope she paid up 10/- like a dutiful wife.

I have just found a letter which I wrote for you about a week ago. I said in it that I'd had a most complete toss just before, landing in my hat and then finding myself none the worse, sitting in the direction in which I'd been going, some yards from the horse who was also lying unhurt. The horse belonged to Bennett Stanford. They are both quite mad (I believe you know Pa B.S. – he's mad too) and it's very nearly uncontrollable but a very good jumper.

The subaltern just senior to me in the battery has applied for the West Coast; he would get about £480 a year and three months leave.

Your loving son,
Arthur

P.S. The P-to-P season is getting quite close and the one-eyed one has bruised his fore foot through casting a shoe. He is being poulticed and anxiously watched by me. It will be rather a sell if he is laid up for a long time.

* * *

Royal Field Artillery, Fermoy.
14th Feb 1914

My dear Mother

We are having the most beastly weather here, very cold and raining or sleeting all day and every day. The country is generally boggy but it is now almost impossible.

We are 'mobilising' (practice only). It's an awful farce. Most of it has to do with imaginary horses & their fodder and the feeding and clothing of imaginary reservists. It practically boils down to an orgy of ink-slinging, without there being any training for the actual thing at all.

We are going to Kildare in the autumn. Far too close to Ulster, I think. It is a two brigade station and the brigade from Shorncliffe is coming there too which includes Jardine who was a great pal of mine at the Shop.

I've bought a horse from someone who was at Charterhouse with me, and in the Yorkshire Light Infantry at Cork. He had left it with a Captain

19

Holroyd-Smyth who is Master of some neighbouring hounds. I went over there and had a hot meal and tried the horse. Smyth hunts in a very long-tailed red coat covered with grease over the collar on which hangs a sort of back fringe of his hair; a pair of nondescript dirty breeches, beneath which there is a hiatus showing his white pants before you get down to his boots which must be seen to be appreciated – likewise his hunting cap. He has 20 horses, most of them thoroughbred, all of them unclipped, which he pressed me to buy in turn, ably seconded by his wife who is a notorious horse-coper.

He belongs to a very old Irish family (descended from Charlemagne or something) and lives in a great big house, half of the windows of which are broken; and half the remainder shuttered up. The family appeared to live in considerable discomfort entirely in the front hall. But they were all very pleasant and hospitable and only too pleased to let me hunt a horse without buying it in the end. There is a certain amount of danger in it, however, as most of the harness is tied together with string.

I'm glad to hear Toby is all right again. I have a fellow-feeling with Molly – horses are a beastly nuisance when they get lame.

> Your loving son
> Arthur

✳   ✳   ✳

. . . There has been a very bad outbreak of foot and mouth disease in Cork county. All hunting has been stopped and nearly all the point-to-points. It's rather annoying as poor old Poly is practically sound and would soon have been fit. There is one more meeting at the beginning of next month which is not cancelled, but I am expecting to hear that it is every day. At any rate I shall be able to tell possible purchasers that he would have won them all if there had been any. Whether they will believe me is another matter.

I'm afraid Ballynor was rather too professional a meeting. The jumps were rather small, thick banks which the chasers took in their stride but which are very 'trappy' for hunters who have been taught to jump on and off. There were fourteen starts. I took a toss at the third bank but caught up the majority of them; when about half way we came to a deep ford where two or three out of each race came down and one horse was killed. There was a hole in it with a steep bank under water the other side. Both Butt and myself were completely immersed; but except for losing a certain amount of skin we're unhurt. We staggered . . .

✳   ✳   ✳

My dear Mother

I should be very glad if you would send me my clothes. Do you remember two silver tumblers which old Duck gave me while I was at Charterhouse? If they are in the house will you send them at the same time?

I have put my old horse in for a point-to-point tomorrow. He is not really eligible as I bought him after February 1st, but as it is a Garrison race I have not told the Secretary of the Hunt, but asked everybody else riding whether they minded. I have been walking round the course today; the banks seemed to grow larger the longer we looked at them.

It is now Wednesday.

We had a great race on Monday and the old horse came in first by about a yard – and I hadn't the confidence to back him though I could have got 10 to 1.

There were nine starters altogether of which only four got round without a toss. The course was about 4 miles long and consisted of banks with ditches on either side, which have to be taken at the gallop, the horse 'changing his feet' on the top, and off again like lightning. I had no experience in this kind of jumping and in the excitement of the moment forgot to keep much of a grip with my knees. So the old horse must be a capital jumper to have gone round without a mistake or a refusal. Of course it was not much of a Meeting but all the best garrison horses were running.

The favourite, a horse called Flittermouse, won the U.H.C. point-to-point. I was riding last for the first three miles and the only people I passed were those lying in a ditch. This happened to Flittermouse no less than three times. The first two times he picked himself up and came harroushing past me again. The third time was the second obstacle from the end when I nearly jumped on his rider's face. Then I had an exciting finish with a Sapper subaltern who is a member of our mess.

The winnings are supposed to be a Garrison Cup and a Sovereign Sweepstake, but I believe the Cup is a myth. But at any rate I shall raise £9 which will fill an aching void. Altogether it was a most amusing experience, but I should imagine you are getting a bit bored with it by this time, but I have to let off steam about it somehow and it is not safe to do it in the mess.

After weighing a savage dashed up to me and seized my saddle and rushed off; I could not find him again for nearly ten minutes which I spent rushing about, cannoning into everyone and blaspheming (I'm sorry to say) while the others were lined up waiting for me. He just arrived in time and I had to gallop up to the starting place.

I hope Miss McKenzie did not lose much.

> Your loving son
> Arthur

*   *   *

Royal Field Artillery, Fermoy.
(Franked April 25 1913.)

My dear Mother

Many thanks for your congratulations. The Garrison Cup, I'm afraid, does not exist, and I am having some difficulty in getting hold of the Sweepstake.

The local tradesmen and horse-copers look upon the officerman as fair game and think it a grievance if he does not like being done for a mug. The draper to whom we all paid our money before the race now declares that it was an entrance fee and that he knows nothing of the sweepstake. However, it was, as a matter of fact, made quite plain to him, originally that it was for the sweepstake. I have got Major Arbuthnot, who commands the other battery and had a horse running in it, to have a go at the man. He was on the race committee and is rather a hard nut to crack.

Dear old Major Wilson has exchanged with a man called Wainwright who is a different sort of person altogether – an ex-Horse Gunner and, they say, rather a terror.

I got the clothes two or three days ago for which many thanks. I hope Molly is none the worse for her accident. I'm glad to hear that the Rent Day was fairly successful.

> Your loving son
> Arthur

Royal Field Artillery Fermoy

*   *   *

My dear Mother

I am trying to think what my next move should be to gain possession of my nine pounds.

When first my long correspondence with Forrest started, our relations were inclined to be strained to say the least of it; we were 'unable to understand'

22

the reasons for anything each other did, and 'called each other's attention' to various things.

But when the Committee decided that the money was to be handed over to me, our reconciliation was quite touching. He couldn't understand how the 'mistake' arose. I thought it the most natural thing in the world! It appeared that we were each the other's ideal of a sportsman and a gent! We thanked one another for our letters and were deeply pained at the trouble and inconvenience we must have caused each other; in fact we were on terms of Oriental politeness. But – this was all more than a week ago and not a sign have I seen or heard about the money. The problem is, shall I continue the mutual admiration business or go back to the beginning again?

There is a lot of talk about our taking over a local pack of harriers. I very much hope we won't as I'm afraid that after my share of the costs have been paid I should be bankrupt and unable to go out with them.

I found a race to put Poly in for, but the course was all for steeplechasers and he was not really as fit as he might have been. But he went well enough to make me quite certain that he would have been a *succes fou* in the ordinary hunt or soldiers' P-to-P, as he can both 'fly' and 'bank' his fences without making a mistake which is an enormous pull in a genuine hunters' race. The race was under the auspices of the C.C.H. of which my friend Holroyd Smyth (who sold me Butt) is Master. The first race was called the Hunt Cup, but was ridden entirely by professionals, the Master's horse being ridden by a well known man called Lombard who rode the winner in all the other three races.

No-one seems to want to pay £40 for Polyphemus.

> Your loving son
> Arthur

* * *

Royal Field Artillery, Fermoy

My dear Father

Yesterday about half a dozen telegrams arrived from brewers and caterers around Kildare, asking for our custom when we go there next autumn. This has spread alarm and despondency in the mess, as Kildare is supposed to be the worst station in Ireland. Everybody is writing off to the brigade who is changing with us to try to get an exchange. My Major (Wainwright) has arranged it already and Carlyon declares that he intends to take on a territorial adjutancy rather than go. I rather think I shall try to go to India if I get an offer from someone who wants to exchange.

I have bought another horse about a week ago. He is sound and has two eyes and seems very fast. Polyphemus has an attack of 'sub-acute laminitis' and is being blistered round the coronet. I hope and pray he will recover in time to be fit for the point to points.

* * *

Royal Field Artillery, Fermoy.

My dear Mother

We have been here nearly a fortnight and leave for Kilworth tomorrow. It has been delightful weather until today, it's pelting now and looks like going on. We shall be in camp continuously until the 19th of Sept. so I hope it does not.

Last Friday we had a night show, 'bivouacking'. Luckily it was a beautiful moonlight night. On Sunday the Army Council had ordered that the Inhabitants were to be amused; so they all ran races etc. and the battery contributed a musical drive à la N. and M. Tournament, and wrestling on horse-back. Two of the guns collided during the drive; that was the star show.

The simple life appears to agree with Polyphemus, but it is rather poor fun cantering one's own horse about these rocky moors. I'm certain to have him lame on me before I've done.

Before Practice Camp we had section, battery, and Brigade training – by subaltern, major and colonel. Now we start Divisional Artillery training under our Brigadier; after which comes Divisional training under the Commander of the whole 6th Division; then the two divisions in the Irish Command have a scrap; and finally the C-in-C takes both of them in hand and manoeuvres them about.

I hope you will be able to read parts of all this.

Your loving son
Arthur

* * *

My dear Mother

We were brought back from Ballyronare yesterday by telegram. I was left in charge of the camp equipment and transport. There were no government vehicles for us and I had an awful day wrestling with a dozen ruffians driving country carts from the camp to the station. There was a battalion of Infantry entraining at the station and no railway people of any sort. Part of our baggage

24

Got everything wanted. Next address Potsdam.

Destination absolutely unknown. Kaiser lives Potsdam. Feeble joke. Sorry.

25

was to be sent to Haulbowline and part to Fermoy and part to Waterford, and when the last country cart rolled up, after stopping for drinks on the way, our train was due in a quarter of an hour. Eventually it all came right as a very casual station master appeared; while the train was three quarters of an hour late.

We have not had any order to mobilise yet, though we expect it at any time; we are all packing up bags and getting them below the weight allowed – 35 lbs in the regimental transport and 100 lbs at the base. As a matter of fact I think that it will be some time before we have to move, if we ever do, as they will never try to transport us as long as Germany has any navy to speak of left. I hope we don't back out of it if there is a general bust-up, as one would imagine that Russia and France would be quite a match for Germany and Austria; I don't believe the Germans are worth much anyway, though they do bounce such a lot.

Many thanks for the cheque!!

I am writing to Harraway who sold me Polyphemus to see if he will buy him back; he would not do as a charger on active service and would be an awful nuisance here without anyone to take an interest in him.

Your loving son
Arthur

John
(Jack)

John (Jack)

L.S.R. Byrne's Esq.
Eton College, Windsor

My dear Mother

I hope you are getting on all right. I saw Arthur at the Field Day which was a very good one. We won. I have hurt my watch and the mending cost is 2/6d, as I am entirely 'broke' do you think you could send it soon, as the man is anxious to see the money!

I think you must inveigle Father over to the Show at Olympia this year, it is going on now & I believe some of the cars are very cheap. You might tell Granny I am doing my exercises regularly & I think my stammering is improving therefrom.

I saw the Kaiser & 'presented arms' in great style. I was standing near the gate through which he came & he had a huge grin on when he passed me, but I believe when he had got to the other end of the line the grin had quite come off & he had a vacant stare on instead. I expect he got rather bored. It was fearfully foggy & he was an hour and a half late so after waiting for about half an hour we were told to lay down our arms & come back in about an hour, so I employed the time in looking at the stables. Some of the horses really are very fine & there are some little Shetland ponies whose heads only come about up to my waist.

You might tell Father, if he doesn't already know, that he had better be careful with the motor when it is in the coach house in case of frosts, as if the water freezes in the pipes & the water jacket it will smash the pipes & perhaps crack the cylinder, so the best way is to empty it out every night.

The holidays don't begin till the 20th so I'm afraid there is 5 weeks yet which is sad. Are you having many frosts? We had our first yesterday & so far it has been very warm here. You must persuade either Dooks or Father to take out the motor or it will be getting rusty, and I insist on being met by the motor when I come from school.

Best love to Father, M., A., C., Bill & yourself.
Best love, your loving son, Jack (!!!)

COMING OF AGE FESTIVITIES AT YOKEFLEET

On Tuesday the village of Yokefleet was quite 'en fête,' when Mr. and Mrs. Empson, Yokefleet Hall, entertained the whole of their tenants, between 300 and 400, to celebrate the coming of age of their eldest son. The morning was very fine, but unfortunately rain fell during the day at intervals, which somewhat marred the pleasure. During the afternoon a cricket match between Married and Single took place. The Benedicts batted first and ran up a score of 64, when rain stopped the play.

One of the principal attractions was to have been the plaiting of the Maypole. The children had been carefully trained by Miss Mackenzie and Misses Hatfield, but the display both in the afternoon and evening was brought to an abrupt conclusion through squalls. A large tent had been erected where the company was provided with tea, over which the wives of the tenant farmers presided.

After tea a greater part of those present assembled in the billiard room, where the 'hero' of the day was presented with a few mementoes. Mr. H. Winn, in a few well-chosen remarks on behalf of the tenant farmers, presented a beautiful half-hunting gold watch and chain, engraved with monogram and crest, and suitably inscribed, and also an illuminated address. The Rev. C. C. Potts, after an amusing speech, gave the cottagers' present—a silver inkstand and candlestick, and Mr. Hatfield wished Mr. Empson, jun., every success in his military career on behalf of the indoor and outdoor staff of the Hall, who had purchased a splendid silver cigar case. The young gentleman was also the recipient of various other gifts, including silver soup tureen from Mr. and Mrs. C. Empson; gold pencil, Capt. Allen-Hoblyn; letter case, Mr. K. Micklethwait; clock, Miss Empson; and a pair of guns, Miss A. Empson.

Mr. John Empson briefly expressed his thanks to the donors for the beautiful presents he had received.

Mr. A. R. Empson, C.C., also expressed his great pleasure at seeing so many present, and hoped they would enjoy themselves, although the rain had partly spoilt their pleasure.

In consequence of the weather an impromptu concert took place in the tent in the evening. The Gilberdyke Brass Band played selections during the day. Messrs. Powles and Briggs, Goole, took various groups of photographs as mementoes of the day.

*   *   *

A party group at Yokefleet Hall.

Plaiting the Maypole.

March 31st 1912   Whittington Barracks
                                                              Lichfield

Dear Father

   At present we are stationed here in Staffordshire in reserve for Strike Duty.
So far we have not actually been on duty in the mines but are in a state of
perpetually standing in readiness in case we may be called on. There are a lot
of mines about 8 miles away in Cannock Chase where the miners have been
rather rowdy & the West Yorks have been called out to look after them.

   As for leave at Easter I am afraid I am very vague about it at present as it
depends entirely on the Strikes. Anyhow I shall not get more than from
Thursday night till Monday night; when do you expect the day's hunting?
I'm afraid the earliest time that we can get away from here is Wednesday so
I'm afraid the prospect of leave looks rather gloomy.

                    Hoping you are all well at home,
                         Your affectionate son,
                              Jack.

                         *   *   *

                         May 15th 1914

                 ARMY FLYING DISASTER.

                 ─────────────

            THREE AEROPLANES WRECKED IN A FOG.

                 ─────────────

            TWO AIRMEN KILLED AND TWO INJURED.

   Disaster befell No. 2 Squadron of the Royal Flying Corps on its way
yesterday from Montrose to Salisbury Plain, three machines being wrecked
in the fog and two airmen killed. Thus four members of the Royal Flying
Corps have met with a tragic death in the course of as many days.

   The night had been spent at Seaton Carew, and early yesterday morning
the ten aeroplanes started on the next stage of the journey from Seaton Carew
to York. They got away without mishap, the morning being beautifully fine.
Passing over the Tees, they flew to the west of the Cleveland and Hambleton
Hills, following closely the line of the Great North Road and the main line of

                              33

Scene from the military funeral, St Clement's, Blacktoft.

the North-Eastern Railway. At the start the conditions were excellent, but about fifteen miles from Seaton Carew a ground mist was encountered, which obscured all the landmarks.

At what time the disaster occurred is not known precisely, as no one appears to have been an actual eye-witness, but about eight o'clock yesterday morning a milkman who obtains his milk from the farm of Mr. William Neasham, Church-lane Farm, Hutton Bonville, some four or six miles north of Northallerton, brought word to the farm that an aeroplane was lying in one of the fields. Mr. Neasham at once went to the spot, and found the aeroplane overturned and smashed to pieces lying in a field and an arm showing underneath. It was clear that the airman was dead, and Neasham hurried away for assistance, and police and doctors were summoned. On returning to the place accompanied by another man he saw the arm of a second man among the wreckage, and when help arrived the aeroplane, which was numbered 331, was lifted, and the bodies of the two men taken out. They proved to be those of Lieutenant Empson and his mechanic, George Cudmore. Death in both cases must have been instantaneous. There were marks which indicated that the aeroplane had descended in a ploughed field, apparently touching ground about ten or twelve yards from a thorn

34

hedge, which separated this field from another at a slightly lower level. Apparently the aeroplane had run forward, caught two or three trees of the hedge, torn them up by the roots, and then turning a somersault had fallen upside-down into the field some three feet below, pinning the two airmen beneath it. The framework was splintered to matchwood, and the wheels of the under-carriage, with the tyres torn off, were lying twenty or thirty yards away.

The bodies of the dead airmen were removed to the house of Harold Beck, miner, in the village of Lovesome Hill, which is only a short distance away from the scene of the accident, and later in the day Major Burke, the commanding officer, appeared on the scene and took charge of the arrangements.

LIEUTENANT RODWELL'S LUCKY ESCAPE.

Meanwhile other serious events were being disclosed. A second aeroplane, No. 332, lay a wreck in a field only a short distance away from Danby Wiske Station of the North-Eastern Railway main line. Fortunately Lieutenant Rodwell and Mechanic William Lee, who were the occupants of this machine,

escaped with nothing more serious than a severe shaking. Lee stated that they flew from West Hartlepool at a height of about 1,000 feet. When about halfway between West Hartlepool and Northallerton they encountered a mist, and could not distinguish the ground beneath them. In the neighbourhood of Danby Wiske they had a little engine trouble, and Lieutenant Rodwell decided to descend. It was difficult, however, as they were unable to tell exactly how near the ground they were until suddenly a tree top loomed out of the mist. To avoid this Lieutenant Rodwell banked to the left, and succeeded in clearing the obstruction, but he had not time to bring the machine back to a level position when the propeller struck the earth. The blades of the propeller were bent backwards, the wings were torn off, and the under-carriage of the aeroplane smashed to pieces. Happily, the airmen themselves escaped serious injury, and scrambled out of their seats. The crash of the machine as it struck the earth was heard some distance away, and the men employed at Danby Wiske Station ran at once to the aid of the airmen. Later in the morning, when the mist had cleared off, Lieutenant Martyn, who was flying Aeroplane No. 235, was seen overhead, and in response to signals he descended safely to the aid of his comrades in distress.

A Third Accident.

Another aeroplane, whose number has not been ascertained, descended in a brickyard near the village of Brompton, two miles from Northallerton. The propeller and some other portions were badly damaged, but the airmen escaped injury. During the morning it was removed to Northallerton Station, where it was placed on a railway waggon for despatch to headquarters.

The news of the series of disasters quickly spread throughout the surrounding country, and cyclists came in from all directions to see the damaged aeroplanes. They were allowed to examine the one at Danby Wiske, but that at Hutton Bonville was carefully guarded by the police, no one being allowed to approach near it until the Government experts have visited the place and made a minute examination to ascertain the cause of the disaster. It is probable that the inquest on the two men killed will be opened at Lovesome Hill this morning.

Lieutenant Empson's Career.

Lieutenant Empson, who was killed, was senior lieutenant of the 7th Royal Fusiliers, and only joined the Flying Corps last December. He was twenty-

three years of age, educated at Eton and Sandhurst, and was the eldest son of
Mr. Arthur Empson, of Yokefleet Hall, Howden. On coming of age he
received several gifts from the tenantry at Yokefleet, Blacktoft, Metham, and
Bishopsoil. He had, since joining the Royal Fusiliers in 1910, taken a great
interest in aviation, and once, when a passenger in a biplane, fell sixty feet,
being, however, only slightly injured. He continued to study aviation. His
parents were awaiting his arrival at York when the news reached them of the
accident.

DANGER OF FLYING IN FOG.

The accidents to members of the Montrose Division of the Royal Flying
Corps were primarily caused, writes our Aeronautical Correspondent, by the
same conditions that cost Britain the life of her first airman at Christmas five
years ago, when Mr. Cecil Grace was drowned in mid-Channel through flying
back from France to England in a fog. There is no doubt that the mishap that
befell Lieutenant Empson and his mechanic would never have occurred had
they had a clear vision of the place on which they were landing. The remark-
able thing is that the members of the Flying Squadron who were forced to

make a landing through mechanical failure, owing to the disconnection of the exhaust pipe of the eight-cylinder engine, got off comparatively lightly.

These accidents unquestionably serve to emphasise the fact that, probably for generations to come, it will be impossible to obviate the dangers of flying through fog. That condition is sufficiently dangerous for shipping, but rocks on the coast can be indicated by buoys with bells, whereas it is impossible to indicate the proximity and contour of land under fog by any system of sound signals. It is equally impossible in those circumstances for a flying machine to continue travelling through the air until the atmosphere clears. That may be a matter of hours, and the fuel supplies are necessarily strictly limited, even if we arrive at the period when it shall be possible for an aeroplane to make a continuous flight of twenty-four hours or more.

The one thing which an aviator cannot do without is vision. This point was brought out two days ago in the evidence given at the inquest on the members of the Royal Flying Corps who were killed in the collision which occurred in mid-air through the comparative absence of a field of vision. Precisely a similar circumstance led to the first serious accident that resulted from a collision of aeroplanes in mid-air. This occurred to Captain Bertram Dickson at the Brescia Flying Meeting some years ago. He was in the act of rising when a monoplane which was descending fell on to his machine, the view beneath him being shut out from the pilot of the descending monoplane, just as the vision behind and above him was denied the pilot of the ascending biplane. Great things, however, have been done lately in the design of aeroplanes for Army use in the way of providing pilot and passenger with the maximum possible range of vision, so that we may take it that in the near future the only possible way of robbing the pilot of his power of vision will be provided by a foggy condition of atmosphere. Already very notable performances have been accomplished in the matter of night flying in ordinarily clear weather conditions, particularly by Commander C. R. Samson, Chief of the Naval Wing of the Royal Flying Corps. But it has not yet been possible to evolve artificial lighting apparatus that can effectively penetrate foggy atmosphere.

Charles

St John's Wood

Charles
St. John's Wood

No 1 Artillery Cadet School
Ordnance Road
St. Johns Wood NW

My dear Mother,

Sorry I have not written before this week but have had to find my feet all over again as we were all suddenly pushed on to St. John's Wood on Friday without any exam or anything. The worst of it is that all my friends in D squad at Handel St. were sent to Lords – where by the way they live like fighting cocks in Pavilion – so I was a bit strange here. In some ways this is an improvement, not so much inspection – none at all today – sheets (!!), the man before probably had them for three months and they were never washed – a fire in the barrack room and more blankets. On the other hand there is more work and things are more terrifying, also the cadets are distinctly a poor lot compared to the last spot. The riding officer's language is much more presentable than my last friend's; however he got quite annoyed this morning and opined that when I rode before it had been in a cart with a net over me. The hours are horribly inconvenient; we are not allowed out of the barracks till 7.30 and must be back by 12.30 – on Saturdays and Sundays however 12.30 to 2.

So far I haven't been able to see the Jerry. I accepted one lunch with him but could not go at the last moment. He goes home every weekend so it is difficult to arrange. At Handel St. last weekend a bloated red hat blew in and I was just shrinking timidly past when it embraced me and turned out to be my uncle Bill! The regimental sergeant major was almost gentle next time he addressed me.

I lunched with the Reynards yesterday and went out with Kenna in the evening. Madge Reynard goes out next Thursday. Mrs de la Fontaine was there too. Kenna looks very fit but uses all her spare breath cursing Americans – why I cannot quite gather as she is having the time of her life. Mrs

43

Meyrick-Wood has also invited me to have a bath any evening I'm feeling like it. (These are practical days, aren't they?) I am applying for leave the first weekend in May but you must understand that it is no certainty; they are fond of cancelling leave for such enormities as blowing one's nose on parade or the loss of a button and I may be caught napping. However I can try. By the way I have not been paid since the last windfall. Must go and do a little stable washing so please thank Molly for my watch.

Your most affection son, Charles.

P.S. The other day a cadet who was on a horse for the first time asked to dismount and move his saddle back as his 'reins were too long'.

* * *

UBIQUE

RFA Officer Cadet School
Ordnance Road
St. Johns Wood NW
Sunday 22nd

My dear Mother,

I am fearfully awed to hear that Arthur is now a captain in an instruction school; especially as his speciality is open warfare which is what we are always being told we shall go out to. Incidentally if the instruction officers here are anything to go by it is an uncommonly good testimonial for Arthur. I spent about half an hour last night putting one of the sergeants to bed; he was a very gentle case. I lit his gas for him and generally tucked him up while he told me lurid and quite untrue tales of his past life. It was really most amusing.

There really is a wonderful collection of people here. I was talking to a man this morning who evidently thought himself a great playwright (don't know his name so he may have been) and explained to me at great length how it's done. The villain of his next piece will be an obvious caricature of Horatio Bottomley (he got acquainted with and studied that gentleman). H. B. will he hopes sue him for libel – there will be much talk and the play will be the catch of the season. Such is modern advertising! I think the man in the next bed to me must have been an Irish music hall bookey sometime in his life: he has the foulest tongue and the sweetest brogue I have met yet.

So sorry Joan has mumps; I shall be most popular if I can spread it here as they could hardly allow less than a fortnight's leave for it. Reveillé is now at 5.30 (N.B. 4.30 by real time) and will soon be at 5. Even Sunday sees us

44

sweeping out stables by 6. On Friday we had stable at 6, 11 and 5 pm, so I'm getting rather fed up with them. The other day one of the sergeants drew me tactfully aside and explained that I needed a new pair of glasses; it seems the old ones were 'orlright for kickin' abaht at 'ome, but not quite the thing for a Tillery Officer. So I now wear pince-nez – and they pince just on the spot that I hit with a steel breech bolt the other day, which is decidedly painful. But I feel I am upholding the honour of the regiment. It is perhaps as well I did get some new ones as the ear things broke off the old pair so I had to keep them up all one day by a piece of sticking plaster across my cheek.

This weekend was pretty well filled again. On Saturday took Mrs St. George to a revue at the Palace, concert and tea at Trocaderos and a cinema (Reggie is right there, and Howard St. George is very bad, I'm afraid). Today, lunched with Aunt Alice and concert at the Albert Hall, where a girl of about 17 named Margaret Fairless played the violin beautifully with full orchestral accompaniment. Bed at 12 Friday night, 5 am till 12.30 pm Saturday, 6 am to goodness knows when tonight is apt to make very sleepy.

Your most affectionate son, Charles.

P.S.   Please don't think I'm dashing about till this hour every night. People are allowed out till then so it is hopeless to try and sleep till the whole room is in.

I don't think there was any question of difference in standard between those sent here and Lords; they simply pushed us in where there was room.

*   *   *

UBIQUE

RFA Officer Cadet School
Ordnance Road
St. Johns Wood NW
Sunday 31/17

My dear Mother,

I was very sorry not to be able to come up to York at Whitsuntide: the military police and 2 guinea railway fare bottled me up in town effectually. However I had quite a good time though sleeping both nights in barracks.

On Sunday I mixed up the Albert Hall and the Palladium concerts. Monday morning 'appy 'ampstead 'eath and was distinctly disappointed; there were crowds and crowds and ranges and cokernut shies, but 'Arry is as extinct as the Dodo. Perhaps the morning was not the best time to go and we were very much on our dignity in glad rags. I went with two dour northcountrymen and simply daren't suggest a ride on a steam roundabout – I suppose such amusements must be classed with pram-wheeling! Then lunch in the Strand, Charlie Chaplin by the way of cheap entertainment, tea at the Troc and a penny seat in the park. In the evening I had an excellent dinner with my prison inspector man and met a great anti-war public hero – Gillingham the parson cricketer: he is a most excellent fellow and not too good at auction. As usual Walter Empson cropped up – he recommended Gillingham for the headmastership of his school in New Zealand and seems to have impressed him very much. We did not play penny points.

You do seem to have your knife into Wood & Co. Poor old thing after taking all that trouble to 'let all men know' his powers, having it all washed out again! I don't think there is any need to worry about the William; he has a large dug-out and Mrs Roderick's family tree to protect him. It does seem to have been a bad raid though: bad enough to wake 'em up and stop it happening again.

I think the odd boot scheme is excellent but please remember that they must have:

    a: no toecaps
    b: no nails underneath and I probably want to dance in them.

But 21s is quite a reasonable price.

Another illusion has been rudely dispelled. I thought, after all these years (!) I had at last learnt to ride but yesterday a lively remount was favoured with a loving embrace from me while taking a jump and I am being 'chased' by the riding man once more. Driving is also rather a sore subject. We seem to have left stables far behind us now which is some comfort. As far as gunnery is concerned field artillery seems easy enough, the difficulty seems to be to get the guns there without carrying away more trees than necessary, or coming into action facing the rear, or neatly snapping off the gate post into the park, or getting all six horses kicking hard with all twelve feet over the traces, or falling off in despair and letting the gun run peaceably over you. I don't know what the park authorities charge the War Office per no. of times my guns come into action. Let's hope they were not very valuable trees!

Give my best love to Grannie, from your most affection son, Charles.

P.S   I am advised to keep away from the front until July 1st so watch for the push now.

*　　*　　*

UBIQUE

No 1 Officers Cadet School RA
Ordnance Road
St. Johns Wood NW
Sunday

My dear Mother,

I am looking forward to seeing you next Saturday and will get weekend all right – but that only means 12.30 am Saturday to 12 midnight Sunday. However it gives me one night out of barracks. I'm afraid it would be impossible to see William off as on weekdays we are only allowed from barracks from 7.30 to 10.30. I may manage to get a pass to see the tailor one day next week and will try and get it while you are in town but that only lets me out after 4 and is considered a tremendous privilege. The army tailor has now taken a month to make my 'glad rags' and there is every prospect of another month elapsing before I really blossom out.

I managed to get in touch with Winnie this week and took her to a show. She seems quite fit and is very hard worked. I believe Di is coming down here sometime next week. I am having a very restful weekend: it is really quite hot today. I got through my first fortnight exam all right so am safe here for another fortnight. We had a very horsey day on Friday. 6–7.30 Stables; 8.45–1.15 Driving Drill on Hampstead Heath; 11.30–1.30 Stables; 2–3 Riding; 3–4 Gun Drill; 5–6.30 Stables. I spent Saturday morning on fatigues – sweeping the Barrack square. Arthur sounds distinctly bored but I should think fairly safe. We are beginning to be rationed quite distinctly and it is rather hungry work.

What are you going to do on Thursday after seeing the William off as I might work the 4 o'clock pass stunt that day? I hope Molly got my letter thanking her for the p.o.s.; it was a wonderful achievement selling that bike. She did pretty well to slay one rabbit at one shot; at that rate her cartridges are not very expensive as 1⅕ d is not much to pay for a rabbit nowadays.

I think they are getting rather anxious to push us through here now so have hopes of getting a commission all right in the long run. There is a fearful uproar here at present among the sergeants as some cadet, name unknown, has complained to his parent with the result that the fatherly war office has sent the C.O. quite a stern letter upon the naughty language used by the instructional sergeants at the cadets. It is really quite uncalled for as the sergeants are mostly very worthy men but it has sent them all on the war path against the conspirator. The commandant is worrying them a good deal too: it is not satisfied with the permanent staff's saluting so they have to parade every day for an hour's marching and saluting drill. You should hear my room

47

orderly on the subject. He is the perfect type of old soldier, by name Pat, has been an N.C.O. and degraded to the ranks ten times and knows about as much about the army as there is to know. Last night he brought us up for inspection the Tillery Uniform he wore in 1882 to emphasise his remarks about 'learning to salute with a lot of conscripts'. The crowning insult was when the head lady at the mess – our feeding is in the hands of some feminine organisation or other, and this lady calls herself lieutenant – told him off for not saluting her. He is very bitter about 'petticoat government'.

I had a ripping dance on Tuesday. The man I was going with could not come so he gave me a letter of introduction to Lady Frances Ryder and I arrived in Grosvenor Place just as the first bomb was dropped (2nd raid). We had a sort of reception there and I signed my name in numerous visitors books and then trotted off en masse to Sir Alfred Mond's house in Lowndes Square. I should think there were two hundred people there and dozens of titles and colonials . . .

From your most affectionate son, Charles.

Arthur

1914–1918

Arthur
1914–18

My dear Mother

I've been getting your letters regularly since you got my battery address but not the ones that went to the base. Another subaltern has joined us – one Easton. He looks just like an entertainer's dummy with an eye-glass and a large long nose but he is very amusing and a gent which is lucky. It means rather less work for the other two of us. We now sleep one at the Infantry Colonel's headquarters, one with the battery and the other in the billet in pyjamas (the last one I mean).

I went down to the Inf. the night before last and was relieved to find a communication trench leading the whole way there (about 6 ft deep) and a very handsomely furnished dugout when I arrived. In the day time one sub. is with the guns, one at the observing station & one goes down to the wagon lines to ginger up the Fairies & Q.M.S.

Things are very quiet hereabouts; they occasionally shell our village with H.E. In fact they have just done so. I was having my hair cut about ten mins. before they started and as the man had not change for 5 fr. I still owe him 2½d. I hope he's not been killed but if he is of course I shall make 2½d. There's a tacit understanding that if they shell us or our Inf. we shell their trenches & vice versa, which has a very quietening effect as of course the Infantry don't thank us for setting it going. This is my day in the O.S. and I'm beginning to wish they would indulge in a little more frightfulness (provided it was nowhere near me) & so give me a chance to 'strafe' them in return & relieve the monotony of this very small barricaded garret. 'Shooting' a battery admittedly beats pheasant shooting hollow, and did not use to come the way of a battery subaltern much.

Some time ago what I believe is a new record was established by a temp. 2nd lieut. in the Div. Am. Col. He was ordered to join a battery. He left the column at 4 o'clock (some 8 miles from the rear) and was a prisoner of war at

8. He had been ordered to report to the Major at the Forward observing station and marched straight to his front with the utmost sang froid, and the first people who took the slightest notice of him were the Germans who apparently bowed him politely into their trench. It happened before my time but apparently he was not popular. In fact Harrison, my captain, says that the German's use of gas was a perfectly justifiable reprisal for our sending them Abrahams.

I hope you're all quite well.
Your loving son, Arthur.

*   *   *

Sunday 20th June   116th Bty   26th Bde   1st Div.

My dear Mother,

This is my third day in the 116th Bty. I joined them at mid-day, and in the middle of the next night we were ordered to be ready to move at once and next morning we came back here which is about half a mile from the Div. Amm. Col. There was very furious cannonading while we were in action and I think our side has the best of it in artillery hereabouts. We shall probably be moved somewhere today.

The two other subalterns in the battery are both temporary: one of them, Lyttleton, was in the navy six years, so they've made him a full Lieutenant. He declares that he was the first temporary officer to come out; there was another one in the same ship as himself (in November) but he (Lyttleton) touched the shore first. I like them both.

It's very hot here but we succeed in keeping fairly comfortable.

I hope you have not been unpleasantly close to a Zeppelin yet; they say here that one was brought down at Hull.

Your loving son,
Arthur.

Passed by Censor No 188   Field Post Office 22nd June 1915

*   *   *

116th Bty   26th Bde   1st Div

My dear Mother,

Thank you very much for the chocolate, I like the Rowntrees sort the best. What I should really like is for *Monsieur mon père* to send me a few good cigars.

I am supping early tonight as I sleep with the Infantry again – the Coldstreams this time, the Scots Guards three days ago. These well known regiments are really quite pathetic. Either an old dugout or an exceptionally young major in charge of the Battalion, a subaltern of about 4 years service for adjutant; quite recently promoted captains in charge of double companies, and the remainder of the officers as far as I can see, mostly under 20 years old.

I am sorry to hear that William is so down in the mouth but his first term will soon be over now.

The latest frightfulness is that we have to arise at 2.30 am from the Inf H.Q.s and repair as best we may to the observing station, what time the rosy-tipped fingers of dewy dawn etc. etc. and there keep watch until 8 am. There's betting as to which of us will be shot first for sleeping at his post. Lubbock is the favourite as he is a very somnolent & indolent sort of fellow. I come next, I don't know why, I'm sure, while Easton who is quite wideawake is a rank outsider.

I saw someone in the Ordnance who was in the 'Erbert * with me. He was full of 'buck' & grievances; he told me of the number of times he had been working under heavy fire and spoke pityingly of the unfortunates who imagined that he was quite safe well in rear of the firing line. I was rather amused as I had felt that way myself when I was in the Div. Amm. Col. where an occasional shell had been known to fall.

> Best love to all
> Your loving son
> Arthur

Passed Censor 188   Field Post Office 13 Jan 1915

*   *   *

116th Bty   26th Bde   1st Division

My dear Mother

I'm afraid it's quite a long time since I wrote last.

I got the cake and it's a great success, thanks very much. I should like a couple of 'fly-strafers' for my birthday; they are made of wire and you flick

---

* The Royal Herbert Military Hospital in Shooters Hill (now being converted into 'desirable residences').

the flies with them. I don't think there is any good sending out money here: I can get as much as I want from the Banque de France or the Field Cashier. I see we are allowed lodging allowance while we are out here which is a free gift as we are not entitled to it. I suppose now that all the little Asquiths & Lloyd-Georges are in the army they have begun to think we were underpaid. At any rate my present takings per diem are 14/- of which I spend about 4/-. I put £50 in the National Loan & find now I could have put a hundred, so I'm rapidly becoming a capitalist.

Easton's section is in a model village belonging to the mine owners about 900 yds. from the German trenches; there is an excellent observing station there, where you can see the German billets & transports miles away to the rear. They put shells through the ground floor of it every now and then and they (Easton & Co) get sniped in certain places. On the other hand he has moved a piano into his house and a choice collection of furniture, and the N.C.O.s have a better mess than they ever have at home. He does not fire, being in reserve in case of attack; & infilading a bit of our zone.

The Major has evolved rather a nice way of protecting our guns. He has put down a light railroad just in front of them and two low wooden trucks to each gun, which is stuffed with earth & sandbags till it is bullet proof; these are kept in front of the guns & can be pushed to either side when the gun has to fire at any particular place. Two or three Generals have looked at it and are quite childish about it. One man is 'detailed' to make a noise like a puff-puff while the S.M. slowly pushes them up & down till the General crows with delight.

Apparently my Regent St. shop did send the parcel to Woolwich, three parcels were sent on from there to the base, none of which have reached me.

Your loving son Arthur

Passed by Censor 188   Field Post Office 27 Jan 1915

*   *   *

July 19th   116th Bty   26th Bde   1st Division

My dear Father

'The situation remains unchanged'! We sighted a Zeppelin, the first I've ever seen, flying behind the German lines yesterday. It was going at an enormous pace and seemed a much less unwieldy affair than I'd always thought.

I'm sitting in what was once a back garden; in front of me is a kind of small rockery with flowers & shrubs planted tastefully on the top of it. At the back is a small opening and inside is a gun. The front of the 'rockery' is open but a piece of canvas painted to represent the surroundings hangs over it, which is pulled up by pulleys from the inside when the gun is to fire. The gun itself is about 3' below the level of the ground, and the rockery is supported by beams. On my right is a house, not quite destroyed, in which is the telephone connected with the Observation Station. It being my day 'at the guns' I have to stay here or hereabouts all day. Of course there is considerable activity when we fire but otherwise it is peaceful to the verge of monotony.

Yes, Botha has done well. I wonder if they are going to send any men here. Or perhaps they will mop up the Deutchers in East Africa first. I am afraid they will be only a drop in the ocean if they come to Europe.

I hope Molly & Miss McKenzie are working very hard at the farm. You must tell them that I am sitting here smoking and thinking how delightfully hot they must be getting. All the French women are working hard.

> Your affectionate son
> Arthur

*   *   *

116th Bty   26th Bde   1st Division

My dear Father

Nothing new has been happening here lately, except that we've been investing in a carpet, a curtain, and some deck chairs for our mess which makes it a good deal more comfortable. From outside it looks barely habitable but inside it's remarkably cosy.

The Germans have taken to shelling our rail-head which means delays in our letters & papers. I've been sending a French Field Service post card home very nearly every day lately; apparently they haven't reached you. I hope you are better now.

I've just had a letter from Cousin Katie in which she said that 'reading between the lines of my last letter' it was obvious that I meant that another advance was coming off; I never had the slightest intention of saying anything of the sort which would have been almost certainly untrue anyway!

> Your affectionate son
> Arthur

* * *

August 26th   116th Bty   26th Bde   1st Division

My dear Mother,

I hope the Zeppelins have not been unpleasantly close again. 'Keep on dodging them' – a form of 'au revoir' used hereabouts – almost applies to you now.

There has been a 'certain activity' the other side of the battery lately and I have been officially awake all night for the last three nights, but have not been called upon to fire. The Germans sent a lot of obus all along our line the day before yesterday, by way of keeping us from rejoicing too much about the Gulf of Riga incident. We sat with great dignity in the observation station for some time until a 5.9 chipped a bit off the corner of the house when we (the telephonist & I) retired hurriedly to the dugout. We found a bit of shell under the table but how it got there I can't make out, as our fortifications were still intact.

The 117th Bty have got an observing station up here now; they have become a 'Counter Battery' and only fire at the enemy's guns, while we fire at their trenches. Also our late attachés from K's army are on their own up here now. I generally go round all of them every day by way of passing the time.

There's a rumour that this division is to go back to rest next week; it will be rather convenient for my leave if they do. I see Brian Palmes has been mentioned again; he has certainly made the most of his opportunities.

Would you please send me out another cake.

The light's getting too bad up here to write so I must finish.

   Your loving son
   Arthur

* * *

August 29th   116th Bty   26th Bde   1st Div

My dear Mother

Apparently the 1st Division is not going to rest after all. We are going to join the rest of the Battery on Friday. I'm glad; though it has been quite amusing up here in some ways, it's rather lonely & a fortnight of it is quite long enough.

A French battery arrived here last night. They don't dig in at all, but plonk down their tin-pot-looking guns by the side of their horses and boost away until they think the Germans have spotted them, then they go off somewhere

56

else & start again. Rather a more exciting method than ours; we've been in Vermelles over two months and have not finished digging yet. However they get caught sometimes; a French battery about 500 yds away lost all four guns by direct hits last week.

We've had some aerial torpedoes the other side of the village. They are very much the same as shells except that they possess wings on the shell instead of rifling in the gun to keep them straight & make no noise when they're coming over – but a very big one when they do arrive.

A 9.2 battery has an observing station a few doors from ours; we've rigged up a telephone wire between them & he rings me up when he is going to fire, which is very seldom, and I go over there & look on. They're bigger guns than any the Germans have near here, and very accurate; there's no difficulty in 'observing' the fall of the shells as they send up a volume of smoke as high as a house.

> Your loving son
> Arthur

P.S.   It's getting very dark; I hope you will be able to read the end of this, as I can't.

Passed by Censor No: 187   Field Post Office 1 Sept 1915

*   *   *

Sept 19th   116th Bty   1st Div.

My dear Father

We haven't had any letters or papers for the last two days, so I suppose something has happened to the mail-boat.

We've just had another subaltern posted to us instead of a Captain, and I am doing the Captain's job for the moment, which mainly consists of looking after the supply of ammunition. Yesterday we had to increase our 'establishment' of ammunition by double, and on paper we were supposed to have any amount of High Explosive. However when we demanded the latter from the 'column', they simply hadn't got any. I hope it will turn up today. Everything seems to point to our being overwhelmingly stronger than the Germans just here and if we don't get through now, I don't know how we are ever going to.

I'm in the observing station now and have just seen quite an extraordinary

57

sight about 1 mile behind the German lines. We saw a flash of light and then a great volume of white smoke coming up for about 30 seconds. I don't want to exaggerate but I think it must be 500 feet high at least. There was very little noise. I suppose it's a mine but whether we have succeeded in exploding it, which seems hardly possible so far behind, or whether it was meant to go off whenever we advance, I don't know. Or it may have been some ammunition store exploding, but one would expect more noise for that. It happened just as I had finished the last paragraph!

Will you ask Mother to send me out another pair of my pyjamas.

I hope you're all well and having a good harvest.

> Your affectionate son
> Arthur

Passed by Censor 188   Field Post Office 22 Sept 1915

* * *

20th Sept.   116th Bty.   26th Bde.   1st Div.

My dear Mother

Thanks very much for the partridges: they were very good.

Nothing very new has been going on here though we are all very busy and everybody optimistic. Twelve of our aeroplanes, all apparently new, flew over here today and went straight over the Bosche lines. About a quarter of an hour later they all came back; what they'd done in the meantime, I can't say.

Poor old Cox's must be overworked: they invariably make two or three mistakes in every account they send me. The other day I sent them a cheque for 50 francs which I'd changed for an attaché. They've just sent a receipt for £50!

> Your loving son
> Arthur

Passed Censor 188   Field Post Office 23 Sept 1915

* * *

Oct 21st

We fired about 1500 rounds of ammunition in the battery yesterday. We were all quite hoarse with shouting & deaf with the noise. We had our 'baptism' of fire but it was the C. of E. method, not total immersion!!

58

No time to write more

Your loving son
Arthur

I got the blanket and the lantern; both very useful. I don't think I want any more underclothes now except socks.

Nov 4th   116th Bty.   26th Bde.   1st Div.

My dear Mother

We are still at rest in the same place; nothing very thrilling has happened since I left except that Lubbock who was due back when I started has not yet turned up.

They kept us a night at Boulogne as the traffic was held up by movements of troops; I believe I could have left a day late without anybody being any the wiser.

I didn't recognise anything in Boulogne till I saw the *Halle des Poissons*, when the geography of the place suddenly came back to me, and I walked straight up the hill to the Hotel de Bourgogne where we stayed about 12 years ago. It was looking a good deal smaller than when I saw it last, but otherwise the same.

There were a lot of Canadian nurses at my hotel; they wore blue cloaks with red linings which were always thrown back over one shoulder and fastened with an enormous gold-looking buckle. Under that they wore a blue tunic with a red gold-laced collar, gilt buttons down the front & a big gilt girdle.

I saw Alice, Katie & Charlie before leaving. I hope they had a good shoot.

Your loving son
Arthur

Passed by Censor No. 188   Field Post Office 6 Nov 1915

*   *   *

116th Bty.   26th Bde.   1st Div.

My dear Mother

I've just received some socks and gloves from Anderson's, for which many thanks; they fit me.

We seem to be almost a fixture here and the Brig. Gen. R.A. has made out a 'scheme of training' for us. It's a good spot and the country round about is interesting to ride about in – hills, woods, old villages etc.

My hostess and servant do their washing together now and their conversation is rather amusing; they seem to understand one another very well, and our farrier who has a figure and character rather like Falstaff's, appears to have established himself as a permanent guest for meals, & invites his pals occasionally. They seem to be a great success, though more with Madame than her Monsieur. This is the sort of thing:

'Vous allez en champagne? (Where a whole British Army is!) Vous?'

'Champagne, Madam (as in English)? Wee, wee, two bottelles par moy every time; tres bong, we won't go home till morning.'

'Ah, vous allez in morning? C'est vrai?'

Etc. etc.

> Your loving son
> Arthur

Field Post Office 11th Nov 1915   Passed Censor No 188

*   *   *

Dec 5th   116th Bty   26th Bde   1st Div.

My dear Father

I'm so sorry to hear you are having trouble with your feet again. Perhaps 'Instructions for Avoiding Trench Feet' would be some use. Whenever a man gets anything wrong with his feet nowadays his Colonel asked for his reasons in writing why (1) his (the man's) socks were not changed more often; (2) why stamping exercises had not been carried out; (3) he had not been warned not to warm his feet when they were cold & wet?

I wrote to Uncle Charlie about a week ago; I talked a lot about the ill-treatment of inventors by the W.O. & the great need for improvement etc. & as little as possible about the actual invention.

My address is at present 4 Quality Street, but I think we shall leave it soon: this is not to be taken to mean that we are about to retreat or advance.

The trenches are very like the warping* just now. The mud reaches up

---

*   Warping – a local term for river silt deposited on land.

about to one's calf but is quite the stickiest stuff I've ever met – like warp that's just beginning to dry.

The worst of Christmas here is that there will be so many letters to censor.

> Your affectionate son
> Arthur

*　*　*

116h Bty.　26th Bde.　1st Div.

My dear Mother,

Nothing very new going on here. There's an absolute maze of trenches in this salient, especially near the sides of it; we hold the same trench as the Germans in two or three places with a 'barrage' in between, and we are still digging new communication trenches, saps, etc.

It's very cold here now – freezing hard with occasional snow, but it's keeping dry still which is a mercy!

It seems rather peculiar not to have starred Dooks at all if his age is 41; rather lucky really.

We gave a dinner party last night with three guests including Lubbock from the 117th Bty with his violin (bring your own mugs).

'They say' that we are all going to Servia but that's only a rumour.

Two true stories from our zone:

1. Colonel X to private of 4th Gloucesters in our second line trench – 'Are you in support here?' (i.e. in reserve).
   Private 'Am I a sport, Sir? Well I 'opes I am, I'm sure'.

2. One Brigadier General Lambert who used to command the 15th Div Artillery had his son Edgar (aged 18) as his orderly officer or A.D.C. Edgar was sent to tell a Battery Commander to take his men to the right side of the road. When he got there he said:
   'Father says you're to move your men to the other side of the road.'
   B.D. (fed up) 'Really, and what does Mother say to that?'

> Your loving son
> Arthur

Passed by Censor No: 188　　　　　　　Field Post Office Nov 29 1915

*　*　*

Jan 21st   116th Bty.   26th Bde.

My dear Mother,

We are still at Auchel and being kept very busy training for the 'moving battle' prophesied in the Spring; they don't talk so much about the coming 'Offensive Action' as much as they did last year. I'm afraid there is no chance of my coming home before February. Graham is on leave now and won't be back for over a week and I am left in charge and even when he comes back either Easton and Harvey should go next. The stylograph has run dry so I'm using a pencil.

Yesterday General Joffre came down and inspected an Infantry Brigade & a Brigade of Artillery. He arrived accompanied by about 30 motors containing various military magnates including Haig whom he invested with an enormous red sash affair. He's a fine looking old man, but rather unsteady on his pins. The inspection was in a very muddy field and the old man came in at one corner and made straight for a wooden platform in the middle; he didn't even glance at the troops on the way, being concerned only with keeping himself on his legs. When he got there, after the Marseillaise had been played, Haig and two other Generals – I think Rawlinson and Wilson – lined up in front of him. He bawled out 'Honneur au General . . . something something something' and put the sash over one of Haig's shoulders, embraced him warmly on either cheek & shook hands; he repeated this with the other two, except that they only got stars. After that he decorated 12 N.C.O.s with the Cross of the Legion of Honour but forebore to embrace them; I thought he might have told off an A.D.C. to do that part for him.

I see they are not going to conscript people till they are eighteen so our Charles will still be a free agent next year. I hope the play was a success. Do you know whether Charley got his watch in the end? I'm sorry the prizes didn't turn up; they were rather good specimens, I have one more and a large piece of the famous Love Tree sawn off as soon as it was cut down.

                Your loving son   Arthur

P.S.   By the way the sailors who were sent on a tour round the trenches came to our part of the line and I saw them as they passed our O.B. It so happened that they struck a really 'hot' day when the Germans had blown up a mine with accompanying frightfulness and they really did lend a hand with rifles and grenades to repulse them. They were tremendously pleased with themselves and their day, but admitted that one day was quite enough.

Passed by Censor 188   Field Post Office 2 Dec 1915

                      *   *   *

October 18th

My dear Mother

I have not been able to send a letter for a long time as there has been no post going and no time for them to be censored. I've written a good many. Peter Saltmarshe must have had a rotten time: I'm afraid we've been getting very much the best of it. At the Aisne it was too mountainous for us to be much use to the Infantry and here it's too flat and woody; but of course we have been fighting in our own peculiar way for a long time. So far I have been more comfortable than on manoeuvres except that we have to do such a lot in the dark and get very little sleep, but of course that's nothing. We can keep dry which is the main thing.

I have been getting your parcels and letters regularly and they are very useful indeed.

We've been billeting in houses and barns lately. The Germans have really behaved very well as a matter of fact though the inhabitants won't admit it. Perhaps they had not much time for loot but they have quite a lot of provisions left. However a town which we have just passed through was very badly pillaged and the church set on fire as an aiming point to their guns. Some of the houses were an extraordinary sight; all the furniture etc. hurled about into the street and the front of them covered with the marks of shrapnel.

A few days ago we stopped most of the day with a French squadron of Cuirassiers. They had lost their supply wagons and had had nothing worth having to eat for three days. We invited the officers to lunch and gave them stewed bully beef, potatoes, cheese, biscuits, bread and jam with vin ordinaire, rum & cigarettes which they seemed pleased to get. They were 'desolated', they said they had an officer who could talk English but he had been killed a few hours before, and also their cook. They had two German prisoners whom they accused of using Dumdum bullets and whom I understand they shot.

There is no harm in saying now that at the [deleted] we were at the top of one high wooded ridge; in front of us was a flat plain 3 miles broad, at the far end of which was the Aisne and then another steep hill where the Germans were. We could stand on our ridge in the woods and see for miles between the armies and their shells bursting; they were actually out of our range and we only fired to get the range etc. to the bridges across the river in case they advanced.

A short time ago before this 'phase' of war had really begun, we all billeted in a large town, dined in a cafe and had a feather bed to sleep in and an omelette for breakfast, but no bath! As I was going to bed my host beckoned me mysteriously into the scullery where Madame and a French interpreter

63

were sitting; he then produced a bottle of excellent champagne and we drank to the Entente Cordiale.

I'm sending this in Father's envelope as your own are with my horse in the wagon lines. We are in our eighth position since the last week and have fired a good deal in all of them except two at quite close ranges, but have not been shelled at all yet, except when they were firing at an aeroplane over our heads and that did not amount to much. I suppose our time will come.

Old Rodin, our fat interpreter, seats himself on one of the 'first-line' wagons which are kept in reserve. However they come up and take the place of the other wagons in an advance, which Rodin did not understand, and so arrived in one position with the guns when we started to fire rapidly – with a basket of looted eggs under his arm. It was an awfully funny sight to see him scooting away to the rear.

I hope this will be over before we've finished all the fruit.

> Your loving son
> Arthur

Passed by Censor 188   Field Post Office Dec 6 1915

*   *   *

Dec 9th   116th Bty.   26th Bde.   1st Div.

My dear Mother

Thanks very much for the pheasants and socks!

Some of my underclothes, notably pants, have been destroyed by shell fire, not 'shot from under me' like Aunt Mabel's groom's six horses, but hanging out to dry after a wash. However most of them have survived but another pair of pants would be quite a good thing.

I'm afraid there is no chance of my getting away for Christmas; the end of January is the first chance. I hope I shall come in for the last day's shooting as I did last year.

I had a letter from Popham yesterday; he gets up for an hour every day but still has a 'tube stuck in his back' which sounds unpleasant; however he appears to be going to survive which is the main thing.

I'm glad to hear that Maud Anderton is going to be married; if you were truly patriotic you would present her with a number of 5/- War Loan vouchers as somebody suggested should have been given to Miss Asquith; but rather trying for everyone to know exactly how much you spent on it. I suppose Dick Pilling will be moved up from Group 3 to Group 30 something but that's spiteful. Do you know where Eric is now? I suppose he's been out for some time.

Please tell Molly that the answer to her question is in the negative – i.e. not quite – but I'm writing to her soon.

> Your loving son
> Arthur

Hoping this finds you etc. etc.

Passed by Censor 138   Field Post Office 11 Dec 1915

*   *   *

Jan 11th   116th Bty.   26th Bde.

My dear Mother

We have been having a lot of fun lately firing at Germans digging in the open, especially at one particular house which is an observing station or else a battalion headquarters and from which they all rush out to a dug-out when we get a shot close to it; and a ridiculous German pipsqueak gun which fires at our bit of trench, gives 'the spice of danger' which they say makes a sport.

We are going to rest for about a month on the 16th unless anything untoward happens not far from where we were at the end of October. I shall be eligible for leave about the 24th but I rather doubt my getting it then as there are others to go first.

I saw Wainewright yesterday who used to command the 34th. He is very pessimistic as usual.

I'm glad to hear McConnell escaped with his life; he would have had a less opinion than ever of 'this 'ere shooting business' if Scruton had peppered him in the legs.

I hope you're all quite well.

> Your loving son
> Arthur

P.S.   I have purchased a Gramophone which warbles to us every evening.

Passed field Censor 388   Field Post Office 14 Jan '16

*   *   *

My dear Father

We came down here to rest last night. for some time we've been supposed to be going, but the incoming gunners could not 'lay out their lines' owing to the fog, so we were left in to hold the line until it cleared, and during that time no post was going.

Easton went on leave this afternoon for a week; he has been out ten months without any leave so he was the obvious one to go first. Only one officer in the battery is allowed at one time and four of us put in our names as 'eligible for and desirous of' it. We have had a new commander issued out to us with other expendable stores on retiring to refit – one Graham, a senior captain. All the Gunner Staff Officers except those actually connected with gunning have been sent back to regimental duty and he is one of the last survivors.

We expect to stay here about ten days. We had good luck in the way of casualties during this last affair; we had a gun hit more than once but it never took longer than 24 hours to put it right again. The other battery in the brigade lost three officers out of five (more or less slightly wounded), a lot of men and 3 guns absolutely knocked out. They were too dashing after the first advance and came under very close fire practically in the open from our left. A good many batteries went on in front of us but they all had to be withdrawn.

I'm glad to hear you had a good Rent Day.

Your affectionate son
Arthur

*   *   *

My dear Father

We move out to rest tonight and tomorrow. I'm going with the first half this evening to the wagon lines and on to our resting place tomorrow afternoon. I'm not sorry to leave this place though it's an interesting part of the line and our casualties have been few; but our observing station was just in the left corner of the salient and we were only about 40 yds. behind the front line, while on our left was a German sap coming to within 30 yds. They have been bringing up trench mortars quite close to us which always cause trouble, and lastly both sides are continually mining and counter-mining. When we come back from rest I believe we've to go further North.

I'm rather afraid that I shan't get leave till February.

66

Can you tell me Aunt Margot's address?

    Your affectionate son
    Arthur

*   *   *

Sunday   116th Bty   26th Bde.   1st Div.

My dear Mother

I have just returned from an open-air service in which a bombardier played the organ. Bosche aeroplanes kept passing over us here, fighting with our own; apparently our 'archies'* have even less effect than they used to, but our aeroplanes bring them down often. One of theirs was hit today just over us but succeeded in 'planing' down to its own lines; occasionally they drop bombs.

The post appears to be slower now both going and coming; I've only just got your letter dated Tuesday, this morning. Our leave has been stopped for a long time but shows signs of starting again.

I hope Molly didn't do anything rash when Dooks revolted.

    Your loving son
    Arthur

Passed by Field Censor 388   Field Post Office 24 Jan 1916

*   *   *

Jan 25th   116th Bty   26th Bde

My dear Father

We are still at the same resting-place. I am at the moment the only officer in the battery and mess with the 117th who have 5 officers! Graham's on leave, Harvey's on a 'course', Easton is doing adjutant and our Serjeant-major has just gone away on promotion. Meanwhile we are supposed to be training very hard; the programme which I have to carry out as acting O.C. is rather amusing, it includes 'training & lectures to young officers.'

Thanks for Aunt Margot's address. It was typical of Cox to pay my allowance into the wrong account. I have just been listening to a detachment

---

* 'Archies' – anti-aircraft batteries.

67

of the maligned R.A. band who have been playing in the market-place; I don't know that I had full value for my three days' pay subscription, but I did what I could although it was raining all the time.

By the way I must apologise for my false information about the Dardenelles some time ago; that's the worst of these Staff Officers; they're so determined to be optimistic that one can believe nothing they say.

Your affectionate son
   Arthur

P.S. A horse of ours died today of colic; attended the [deleted by censor] post-mortem; his inside was absolutely chock full of sand and dirt.

Passed Field Censor 388   Field Post Office 27 Jan 1916

     * * *

          116th Bty. 26th Bde. 1st Div.

My dear Mother

Graham has just returned (before dinner) and I have spent a bad half hour in the confessionary: item one horse dead; do. quartermaster sergeant found drunk in a neighbouring village by military police etc. etc. I am putting in leave for next Wednesday which I may or may not get, if so I shall probably be home on Friday evening. I went to a concert the other night in Lillers which was quite good. A gentleman of the name of Romford who is apparently a great man sang.

We are going on 'Manoeuvres' this next week; one of its objects is to be rapid billeting under service conditions by Divisional staff – which means making everybody deliberately uncomfortable. I trust they don't stop my leave for it.

Looking forward to seeing you again.

  Your loving son
   Arthur

Passed Field Censor 388   Field Post Office 1 Feb 1916

     * * *

                Same address

My dear Father

La Lutte, rude et acharnée as the French papers call it, against the mud, still continues. Yesterday the enemy attacked in force after a prolonged bombard-

68

ment of snow and carried our advance 'soakpit' at the point of the bayonet; our brave soldiers undaunted were engaged in launching a counter-attack from another soakpit further back when we were most treacherously attacked in the rear by a General who suspected our efforts and solemnly said that much might be done by putting down shale from the mines and by digging drains – which is what we've been doing since we arrived.

No thanks very much. I've got all the warm clothes I want. The news from Verdun seems good; if they get beaten this time we really ought to be able to take the initiative at last and start harrying them.

> Your affectionate son
> Arthur

Passed field Censor 388   Field Post Office 28 Feb 1916

(Arthur's father died in March 1916.)

POST OFFICE TELEGRAPHS

O.H.M.S. War Office London   Blacktoft
                                                22 August 1916
To: Empson Yokefleet Hall Howden.

Regret to inform you that Lieut. A. Empson R.F.A. was wounded August 18. Further details sent when received.

> Secretary   War Office.

✳   ✳   ✳

My dear Mother

They have at last discovered the bit of shrapnel and have made a gallant attempt to extract it this morning but without any success; so I have to have what old man Smith calls a whiff tomorrow morning. I'm afraid this puts back the date of my leaving hospital for at least another week if not ten days. However, I am going to the pitch this afternoon.

I wrote Charlie's letter last Saturday but forgot to post it.

> Your loving son
> Arthur

Sister Watson is going to be married which explains her recklessness in turning out the Colonel's wife.

NOTHING is to be written on this side except the date and signature of the sender. Sentences not required may be erased. **If anything else is added the post card will be destroyed.**

I am quite well.

I have been admitted into hospital

$\left\{ \begin{array}{l} \textit{sick} \\ \textit{wounded} \end{array} \right\}$ *and am going on well.*
and hope to be discharged soon.

I am being sent down to the base.

I have received your $\left\{ \begin{array}{l} \textit{letter dated}\underline{\hspace{3cm}} \\ \textit{telegram ,,}\underline{\hspace{2.5cm}} \\ \textit{parcel ,,}\underline{\hspace{2.5cm}} \end{array} \right.$

Letter follows at first opportunity.

I have received no letter from you
$\left\{ \begin{array}{l} \textit{lately.} \\ \textit{for a long time.} \end{array} \right.$

Signature $\left.\begin{array}{l} \\ \end{array}\right\}$
only.

*Date*_____

[Postage must be prepaid on any letter or post card addressed to the sender of this card.]

(93509) Wt. W3497-293 1,125m. 5/16 J. J. K. & Co., Ltd.

70

* * *

Y.M.C.A.
c/o Town Major
Arras
B.E.F.

September 9 1916

Dear Mrs. Empson,

I was very sorry to see in the *Daily Mail* Arthur's name among the wounded.

I do hope not seriously & that he is going on well. Is he in England? I have asked Charlie to let me have a line to say how he is.

It is a sad and anxious time for you.

Would you kindly give the enclosed to Charlie.

I hope to get home beginning of October.

> Yours sincerely,
> P.W. Lloyd.

* * *

Royal Herbert Hospital, Woolwich

Dear Molly

Thanks very much for your letters with all the local scandal. I didn't get one from you at the front; perhaps it will arrive here soon. I still have to lie nearly flat so that I don't write much. I hope that you are having a good time and that the pony is behaving well.

My wound is quite healed up and I don't have any bandages on it at all. But I still cough and give out the wrong noises when my chest is tapped; but I'm getting better altogether quite quickly and expect to be allowed to sit up quite soon.

Charles came to see me a short time ago. They are having lots of field days & route marches at Harrow, but I was too sleepy at the time to hear much.

Just before I was wounded we were close to a farm house where we used to sleep when we got a chance, and two girls had stayed there to look after things. Nothing would induce them to go away, although two shells burst right into the house, one into the kitchen, and made an awful mess. But they were still determined that we should not burn more than 2 of the drawing room candles at a time; we slept in the drawing room and she used to come in and put them out if she saw more burning.

> Your affectionate brother
> Arthur

* * *

26th Bde   R.F.A.   1st Division

Dear Aunt Ethel

Thank you for your letter. I never quite know myself whether I'm working or resting; on the whole I think I get through my eight hour day, but it is work which I personally find a pleasant change to the trenches, especially after our last position which was in just about the worst bit of the line for the . . . d Gunners. Nowadays I potter about, prod horses in the stomach and put them on bran instead of oats etc. and tell Dr. Snooks to get his hair cut. I also answer conundrums about the quantity of raspberry jam & 'pins, linch, safety for wagon ammunition Mach 2' which I received last Tuesday.

We are having delightful weather here; very hot but no flies around yet; I'm afraid they won't be long in coming however.

What are they going to do to Casement? Shoot him, I hope, but they'll make trouble in Ireland if they do, don't you think so?

I'm afraid I've been very unsuccessful in getting 'souvenirs' home. I've made a good many attempts with fuses but always failed, and German badges are rather hard to find.

I hope you are all quite well in spite of this hard work! Please excuse this appalling writing.

> Yours very sincerely,
> Arthur Empson

P.S.   I'm sorry to hear that Charlie is on such a low moral plane. I remember going to the cinema with Aunt Nellie & Lucy when a distinctly risqué thing called 'Shop Girls' was filmed. The Aunt divided her time between explaining to Lucy how silly it all was & how she couldn't understand what they meant, and telling me what an important social question it all was and what a lot of good these films did. As we both heard what she said to the other, it must have been rather puzzling to Lucy . . . [deleted by censor].

72

*   *   *

116th Bty   26th Bde   1st Division

My dear Mother

I've just had a letter from Molly, apparently she is a fag! and remarks that her hands are smarting through doing fielding-practice!! I had no idea that Girls' Schools went in for all that sort of thing, but it ought to suit Molly.

We have sent a detached section away some miles south, which I am in charge of. We are in what must have been an awfully nice estate; it's a big wood on a ridge; the chateau is absolutely destroyed as you may imagine, as the French front line ran just behind it a year ago; it had been going for about 1000 years (parts of it, that is) before that; there is rather a fine lake just by it but unfortunately that is visible from the German lines. My bedroom and mess combined, which is a small dugout, said to be proof against anything, is made against the ruins of the late Monsieur le Comte's mausoleum – rather a quaint practice, being buried at the bottom of your garden – he died at the age of 92 in 1913; he was rather lucky not to live a year longer.

When the position was handed over to me, my predecessor told me that he had a beautiful observing station and led me to one of the largest trees I've ever seen, up which some very rickety ladders were laid; we climbed up and up until at the very top we came to a perch with only room for one. This did not daunt my guide; he balanced himself on a very flimsy branch and waving airily towards the trenches said 'Of course you see our 'Zero line''; I paused a minute before replying as I was at the moment being violently sick – there was a high wind and I hesitate to say how high the tree was – and then retorted, I'm afraid with a certain amount of irritation, that I did not, but if he would wait a minute and then put the telescope on the exact spot, I'd no doubt I should.

I've no time to write any more, hoping you are very well.

> Your loving son
> Arthur

*   *   *

116th Bty   26th Bde   1st Division

My dear Mother

What on earth did Nellie Palmes spend all her money on! I trust Aunt Margot isn't a dark horse of that sort too; it would be very trying, wouldn't

73

it? If she were, what dissipation can she be going in for, secretly, besides lecterns? I wonder. I think the lectern is a good idea, perhaps I ought to offer to pay half of it, but of course I really don't know what money I shall have yet. As Islington refuses to pay Uncle Charlie's income tax, I've had to pay for the half year out of my Cox's account.

Molly tells me that she is a fag which she pretends to enjoy, and also that her hands were smarting after fielding practice – certainly a go-ahead school.

Nothing very new here; there is a certain amount of shelling going on but we've dug down so deeply now that it makes very little difference to us.

> Your loving son
> Arthur

*　　*　　*

4th Army Artillery School　B.E.F.

My dear Mother

I arrived here the day before yesterday after two days' march; we stopped the night at a small village, arriving in a hail-storm. We had quite good billets but realised the appalling shortage of coal among the civilian population in France.

I lodged with the priest and spent the evening talking with him in pigeon French. He is a pessimist about his own profession, and says that all the priests in Russia will be getting guillotined soon, and that atheism will be worse than ever in France after the war. Apparently, although the church is the most obvious building in every village, the 'free thinkers' hereabouts have it all their own way and make it hot for the elect; as the old man said – 'In France we write Liberty on our walls, but it exists nowhere.'

My job here consists in 'turning out' guns & gun teams etc. spotlessly clean to astonish the young officer taking the course; and in my spare time to teach gun drill to the section.

It's quite easy work and very civilised conditions.

> Your loving son
> Arthur

*　　*　　*

51st Bty　39th Bde R.F.A.　B.E.F.

My dear Mother

I'm afraid my account of the 'great advance' has been dull, but as a matter of

74

fact, except that we were in Bosche territory and, as I said, cantering about instead of slushing along trenches, it was a very tame affair; we knew it was coming for a long time as we could see the villages burning behind, though he held his front line strongly. Then one day he disappeared, and we apparently made little or no attempt to keep up with him; there were reasons for this which the censor would not pass. One officer was cut about the face by a bomb partially exploding in the fire in their new mess dugout and of course we brought all our water with us; otherwise we met none of those superhuman traps that he was supposed to be preparing (subterranean mines etc.) I don't know what cavalry were out in front of us except that an infantry friend of mine told me that they were not really cavalry, but only yeomanry – he was a bold bad man!

At present we are busy training for the 'warfare of the future' – not of the next war, they're not quite as optimistic as all that; they only mean that our side will not allow the thing to degenerate into trench warfare any more. I frankly don't believe a word of it. I feel convinced that we shall have a long line of defences further back to bash through in a steady old Somme-ish way.

I sent you a card sent me by Easton yesterday; I don't know who the artist was, perhaps a recent importation. It was rather eccentrically addressed, as I had to use the same envelope.

> Must stop & go to bed.
> Your loving son
> Arthur

*   *   *

4th Army Artillery School   B.E.F.

My dear Mother

I'm glad the card reached you. It is supposed to represent the 4 different years in which the battery has been out here; 1914 in the top left hand corner (the retreat); 1915 underneath, showing Ypres and the slag heaps at Loos; 1916 in the bottom right hand corner by the tanks & Albert Church; 1917 by Time with rather a jagged looking scythe. The remark in the middle is by Easton, and is a favourite saying of the men. For instance, if Driver Jones writes to his best girl and says 'Roll on a very long time' he doesn't mean that the lady is to go in for gymnastics, but is addressing the 'terrestrial orb' or Time, or something of the sort.

Since I haven't mentioned their number or the division I may say that they sent it round on leaving our division and will be in the thick of the real fighting now –

Easton's card.

confound them. We have just got the first news here by official wire, probably you will know all about it by this time. I feel very sick at being here while it's going on; I've been in all the real 'pushes' so far and I'm afraid our days unopposed advance of a fortnight ago hardly counts. But as it is snowing hard today, there are consolations in not being in it! It looks from what we know at present to be the real thing. I suppose the Germans will try to take Petrograd.

I hope you and Grannie are quite well again now and wrestling with the food controller all right.

> Your loving son
> Arthur

We had a cross-country run yesterday 1 mile and a half <u>120</u> starters; I came in 4th, which shows there is nothing wrong with me now.

> 116th Bty   26th Bd   1st Div.

My dear Mother

I'm sorry to hear that William has whooping cough; I suppose Molly's half term holiday is over now.

I am writing this after a midnight raid, my part in which was to sit in my tree and time my guns firing on their various targets; the Gunner staff have got this sort of thing down to a fine art now. Three days ago I received a tracing from an aeroplane photo of our trenches with the positions which I was to shell at various 'periods' marked in red ink. These I registered by firing discreetly on them one or two days before the strafe. They also give me a timetable, for instance:

0–0.5 Target A on map attacked – 2 guns – intense – 80 rounds – High Explosive.

0.5–0.25 Lift to Target B – steady rate of fire – 60 rounds – H.E. – 30 Shrapnel etc.

0 is a certain time which is not divulged until about an hour before the curtain is rung up; so that everybody taking part knows all that he has to do and what is going to happen three days beforehand, except the time; on this occasion it was 11.10 pm! Of course the first five minutes we thoroughly strafe their front lines while the infantry crawl up on their tums as close as they dare; at 0.5 they dash into the German trenches while we 'lift' our fire onto the communications support trenches. The raiding party have about 25 minutes in the trench in which they throw bombs into all the dugouts, take as many prisoners as they can to get information from them, and bayonet all they can't; but their object is generally to spoil the Bosche mining arrangements or to capture a machine gun or two, or a trench mortar. They're also expected to come away with a new pattern of German smoke helmet, and complete evidence as to what Corps is opposing us. So they have their work cut out!! Then they shuttle back again and all is peace once more. It looked like fireworks from my tree.

Do you see that I only have to pay the old rate of income tax?

Your loving son
Arthur

*   *   *

July 31st   116th Bty   26th Bde   1st Division
My dear Mother

Thanks very much for your letter. Everything is going on very much the same here. We had a little shell dodging to do the day before yesterday but we avoided them successfully. Really one begins to feel the greatest contempt for shells after a bit; if you do get caught in the open & lie down flat whenever you hear one coming, the odds are on your side even when quite a big one

77

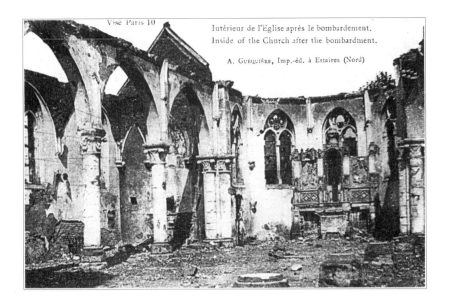

bursts within 20 yards of you. It's extraordinary the amount of metal sent into this village without doing any appreciable damage, I mean during the whole time that the firing line has been close to it.

Our captain has just left the battery & another one – Boscowen – has come instead. Harrison (the former one) was very small & truculent. He & Lubbock and myself were walking along a few days ago when we saw a light flashing in a window about half a mile away, so the little man set off at a tremendous pace, thinking that this was a spy signalling. When we caught him up he was in the wrong house, and trying to explain his trouble to a French family. His French is 'heroic' at the best of times and he was very much out of breath; so that he was getting more and more abusive to Monsieur who remained very polite all the time, but when we succeeded in explaining to Harrison that it was the next house & he started to apologise, the Frenchman said, still very politely, that for his part he found M'sieu. le Capitaine more worthy of pity than blame, which I thought was rather good. The next house was an Officers' billet with a lamp on the table close to the window & an orderly laying the table who kept passing to and fro in front of the lamp. So the little man had to retire baulked of his prey.

I should like my birthday presents to be strictly useful. My demands are as follows:

  2 flystrafers
  6 handkerchiefs
  3 pr of socks
  2 pr of thin pants

A hamper containing

  1 tongue
  Some potted meat
  1 cake
  1 tin of lunch biscuits
  Some chocolate

I'm not in the least hurry for any of these things, so when you are next in York or Hull will do.

Hoping you are all quite well still.

  Your loving son
  Arthur

*　　*　　*

Saturday June 12th   No 2 General Base Depot Havre

My dear Father

I have just returned here after three days absence and find that not a single officer has been sent up from here while I've been away.

I had to take 50 drivers and 50 gunners to a place called Abbeville and 'return on completion'. None of them deserted or got lost. Abbeville is a long way from the firing line and I couldn't even hear the big guns from there. It would have been quite amusing if it had not been so very hot and uncomfortable; but we started off with a seven mile march in the sweltering heat and then had to sleep three nights in the train. When we got to the station at Havre I found that our train did not go for 7 hours – 12.30 at night – and I did not like to leave the men as it's very likely for one or two of them to make up their minds that Nature didn't intend them for ''eroes', and I imagine that you are not exactly thanked if you turn up with fewer men than you started with.

We have had a thunderstorm here which has cleared the air considerably.

The only duty we have to perform in the camp is censoring letters and as the men have nothing much to do either, they spend most of their time writing them. One man wrote four letters, all very affectionate and exactly the same, to four different girls; another one let on that he was in the trenches and described the horrors of war in the most picturesque terms.

> Your affectionate son
> Arthur

Passed Field Censor 300

*　*　*

26th Bde R.F.A.　1st Division

My dear Mother

I'm sorry there has been such a gap in my correspondence; I've been very busy lately and have not much time to write now.

I'm very glad to hear that you are getting everything settled. I shouldn't mind selling any of the foals if one could get a proper price for them; they will (especially the eldest) be rather a nuisance if we've got no one to break them in.

It's a most extraordinary thing that I never knew that Colonel Saltmarshe was attached to our Headquarters. I asked our Adjutant and he said that he was there for three days some time ago; what made it more funny is that a subaltern in the 117th told me some time ago that while he was 'observing' he heard a 'roar like a bull' and an 'enormous dug-out colonel' had appeared who sat down before the observation window, swept off the instruments from the ledge, and demanded to know which were the German trenches & which were ours, at the same time pushing the end of the telescope out of the window (a crime as it may give the place away). Driscoll also said that when he had recovered from his astonishment and talked with him, he thought him a 'dear old thing really'; and it never occurred to me who it was!!

When do you intend to move? And are you going to Granny first?

> Your loving son
> Arthur

*　*　*

116th Bty　26th Bde　1st Div

My dear Mother

Thanks very much for the fly cream & writing paper. Yes, I've got Aunt

80

Margot's puggaree and wrote to thank her for it. I've just had a letter from Uncle Charlie which he addressed to 34th Bty. It went there first, then on to the 'Erbert, then to Cox's and so here. Pretty good on the part of the postal service, I think.

I daresay the Russian situation makes them expect a big attack soon. We can't go on like this for ever, I suppose. At present there is very little going on here. 'Reprisals' (2 shells to their 1) are the order of the day still. Lubbock has the ghost of a camera, not a real one of course; that's strictly against regulations. He took some very good ones of our last position (where I was 12 hours) & has promised to tell his wife to send you some of them.

There has been a good deal of firing on our right lately where the . . . have been fighting very hard just lately. There was a French 7.5 battery quite close to us until a few days ago and we had great fun with them. One M'sieu le Capitain Jambon commanded them; he accosted the Major & remarked that he had a battery 'qui marche tres bien' & asked him to come & see it; all he showed him as a matter of fact was the mess which marched very bien.

Could you send me out a fairly large cake for the mess, rather of the plum pudding variety.

> Your loving son
> Arthur

*   *   *

My dear Mother

We have struck a very comfortable billet here in a large farm, after a short sharp scrap which, including all preliminaries, lasted 3 weeks. It was certainly a great success and went off without a hitch; I understand it is part of a bigger scheme of attack than has yet been tried on the Western Front. It's a much more satisfactory way of fighting than continued trench warfare.

I see that Mr. Lloyd George could hear the mines at Walton Heath;* I was within 600 yds of the main one and had some difficulty in hearing anything else for about twelve hours, but I shall be running up against the censor soon.

I'm sending you another letter from Wood: he apparently is not very annoyed at my cancelling the thing-me-jig, though a little dignified. It's rather typical of him not to say which mortgage is on the Reedness farm. I feel sure

---

* At 3.10 on the morning of 7th June 1917 the mines were all set off at once at Messines. According to A.J.P. Taylor, Lloyd George heard them in No. 10.

that he is honest, though I daresay he drinks, but my complaint against him is his policy of – 'darkness & not much composure'; it seems almost impossible to get all the facts out of him, because of course he would have less to do then.

I'm glad to hear that you are going to Yokefleet for a bit and hope you will have decent weather.

Your loving son
Arthur

Passed Field Censor 4692   Field Post Office 14 July 1917

51st Battery

My dear Mother

It has been very hot here all day with lightning and a little thunder in the distance & no wind; suddenly at 4 o'clock a hurricane started and went on for half an hour. It didn't actually blow a tree down but it might very well have done & now an hour later it's absolutely still again and no rain which is rather a pity as there is likely to be a drought.

We (the Divisional Artillery) who were 'covering' strange infantry have had no end of good chits etc. In fact one Brigadier went so far as to say that his men would go to <u>Hell</u> behind our barrage which is about where they do go, poor fellows. They certainly get the worst of it every time and the good feeling between us is very creditable to them, but I'm afraid that if we have any open warfare and these tremendous barrages cannot be arranged by the clock, they will rather resent it.

I had my first strawberries & cream since the war started yesterday; our Madame has a large garden of them and 40 cows which she and another woman, who is obviously a companion, help to milk.

Your loving son
Arthur

∗   ∗   ∗

29–7–17   51st Bty   39th Bde R.F.A.   B.E.F.

My dear Mother

Thanks very much for 'knife, fork & 'poon – what my godfathers and godmothers did for me at my baptism'. They are very useful.

I hope it will be more peaceful next year; I'm afraid the financial situation will be very bad if it does not. The *Daily Mail Continental* cheerfully remarks that if we can only hold out till next year when the Yanks will be in, all may yet be well. Surely this is a pessimistic view of the general situation!

I don't see much big German offensive doing any good against us and I think his best chance is to withdraw to prepared lines some way behind whenever he sees – as he always can see – our big push preparations are complete, which would mean our starting them all over again with a small gain of territory.

I am rolling on as usual, getting very much in need of a little leave to break the monotony and get a little exercise. Now that our friend has kindly come to within twelve hundred yards of us we don't even have to walk up to an Observing Post, and as useless walking about in the open is deprecated for more reasons than one, we spend most of the time underground growing fatter & fatter.

> Your loving son
> Arthur

*　　*　　*

Post Office Telegraphs

Office of Origin and Service Instructions   *Office Stamp*

O.H.M.S. War Office London.   Blacktoft

23 August 1917

To: Empson Yokefleet Hall Howden Yorks.

Deeply regret to inform you that Lieut. A. Empson R.F.A. 296th Brigade was killed in action August 21st. The Army Council express their sympathy.

Secretary   War Office

O.H.M.S. War Office London.   Blacktoft

24 August 1917

Re your telegram today. Lieut. A. Empson R.F.A. 296 Brigade. Only one A. Empson in Army List. Number of Brigade given as reported by D.A.G. Base.

Secretary   War Office

Kings Cross Station   Blacktoft
                                                25th August 1917

List not in. They have promised to wire immediately. Home tonight.

                                                        Charlie.

O.H.M.S. War Office London.   Blacktoft
                                                29th August 1917

Lt. A. Empson reported 296th Brigade. Division and Battery not known.

                                          Secretary   War Office

O.H.M.S. War Office   Blacktoft
                                                30 August 1917

Your letter received. Enquiries being made to Base. Will communicate
reply immediately received.

                                          Secretary   War Office

O.H.M.S. War Office   Blacktoft
                                                31 August 1917

4278 Ag 6 30.8.17 aaa. Reference your wire 27th inst. 51st Battery 39th
Brigade R.F.A. 1st Division B.E.F.

                                                      Seemliness

Cf. Last night. Buckingham Palace.   Blacktoft
                                                5 September 1917

The King & Queen deeply regret the loss you and the Army have sustained
by the death of your son in the service of his country. Their Majesties truly
sympathise with you in your sorrow.

                                          Keeper of the Privy Purse.

O.H.M.S. War Office   Blacktoft
                                              9 September 1917

Enquiries being made. Letter despatched to Cadet Empson today.

                                        Secretary   War Office

O.H.M.S. War Office   Blacktoft
                                             11 September 1917

Glad to inform you that report of death of Lieut A. Empson incorrect.
Letter follows.

                                        Secretary   War Office

Cf. Last Night. O.H.M.S. Buckingham Palace.   Blacktoft
                                             18 September 1917

I regret delay in answering your letter as it was necessary to await full
particulars from Headquarters in France. The King and Queen have heard
with much pleasure that your son who was officially reported killed, by
mistake, is alive, and their Majesties rejoice with you at the good news which
they know must be such a great relief to you and your Husband.

          Ponsonby   Keeper of His Majesty's Privy Purse

                    *   *   *

          Saltmarshe, Howden, Yorkshire.

                                                  August 26.

Dear Mrs. Empson

I find it difficult to tell you how deeply I feel for you in your great
bereavement, and do trust that you will find some consolation in the fact that
poor Arthur has met with a soldier's death after serving his country so
gallantly for three years.

I always felt so much interest in him not only as a neighbour but a member
of my old corps, and was much disappointed that I did not see him when last
at home.

His father and I were friends from childhood, and I looked forward to a

85

continuation of this friendship with Arthur, a friendship which I trusted would always exist between him and my boy after I am gone.

Believe me we are all sorrowing for you and yours today.

Yours very sincerely,

P. Saltmarshe.

To: Mrs. Empson, Yokefleet Hall, Howden, E. Yorks.

* * *

14th Sept   51st Bty.

My dear Mother

Just a line to let you know that if anybody has been reporting me dead, missing or sick lately, he is misinformed.

I wrote to Biggs some time ago but have had no reply. I suppose he is waiting to hear from Hillas or somebody.

We are very busy with concrete etc. etc. 'against' the winter.

Rather a good move of the King to send telegrams of condolence to all the next of kin! Earning his salary, I suppose.

Please give my love to Grannie; I hope you are all quite well.

Your loving son
Arthur

* * *

5th Oct.   116th Bty.
                                                                                                        26th Bde.
                                                                                                        1st Dvn.

My dear Mother,

There is a lull here just now, so we are to go down to the wagon lines for three nights in order to look after the men, horses etc. there. I'm starting tonight. I'm looking forward to a bath, a hair cut and dry clothes. Also it's a good three miles back so one gets away from these shells for a bit. Our highly efficient Sergeant Major used to live there permanently but he is going to take a commission.

We've had extraordinary few casualties in this battery, the major being the only officer hit. The other battery lost three out of five. The trouble was that we are in a salient here and batteries were pushed up in support of their own

86

M.S.3. (Cas.)

8th September, 1917.

Dear Sir,

In reply to your letter of the 6th September, regarding your brother, Lieutenant A. Empson, Royal Field Artillery, we have made a special enquiry to find out why he is reported killed, as it seems evident, from what you say, that the report was rendered in error.

I understand from your letter that your brother's letters were dated by him after his reported death and that the dates referred to by you are not post marks.

I am exceedingly sorry that your parents should have had all this anxiety, but there is no doubt that the official report definitely stated that he had been killed on the 21st.

Directly I get any information I will write at once to Mr. Empson.

I am, Yours faithfully,

H. [signature]

Captain,
for Military Secretary.

Cadet C. Empson.

India Office.

Whitehall, S.W. 1.

14th September, 1917.

Dear Mrs. Empson,

I am sorry to say that owing to being laid up I have been prevented till to-day from making any enquiries from the War Office about your son. The War Office tell me that the whole thing is a mistake made in France. They have, I understand, at last let you know, and I believe the Military Secretary, Sir Francis Davies, is himself writing to you to-day to apologise for what has happened. They say that an official correcting notice will appear in the Press about Wednesday next. I sympathise with you most deeply for the dreadful anxiety through which you must have passed.

But how relieved you must feel now.

Yours sincerely,

[signature] Islington

Mrs. Empson,

infantry in front without any regard to the enfilade fire from either flank, but it's been found impossible to help them there.

It's been rather disappointing after the first day, but I suppose we shall get on again soon, at any rate I don't think we shall continue to hold the line as it is at present and if we could take their strong-hold on our left we should be in quite a strong position.

The bombardment and the first attack was [?] excellently but there seems to be not enough reinforcements to carry on the good work and some of them came up without food either inside them or outside and that doesn't do when it's a question of dislodging Brother Bosche.

I forgot to thank you for the nice lot of partridges; they arrived at a very opportune moment when the mess cook was wondering how to carry on without a stove. They were rather high as a matter of fact but quite eatable.

If Charly goes to Woolwich in November he will be probably out of it in May and will then most probably go to a battery at home; at least no subalterns come out to us straight from the shop. Of course when the war is over his varsity and civil service career will be upset, but most other people will be in the same boat. Easton says he was doing fourteen hours cramming a day to get into the diplomatic, and has now forgotten everything.

The whole battery or the part of it that lives up here has dug itself into this disused trench, the latter making a sort of long corridor. We have four apartments at various depths,

Your loving son, Arthur.

P.S.   I got the shirt, socks and chocolate for which many thanks. I consumed most of it yesterday during an otherwise cheerless day in the trenches observing.

* * *

8-10-17   51st Bty   39th Bde. R.F.A.

My dear Mother

We have just altered our time to the winter variety. I had been looking forward to an extra hour in bed, but it just happened to be my turn at 'Night O.P.' which consists of gazing at the darkness from 7pm to 6am; if the Infantry are attacked they send up a rocket or something of the sort, and I have a rifle with the same sort of rocket which I buzz off if the other thing goes up, meanwhile sending S.O.S. with approx. position of same to the various batteries by telephone. After a suitable interval they all blaze away at prearranged points on which the guns are already laid. Very thrilling if & while it

88

happens, but does not make up for the boredom of the rest of the night. So you can imagine how much it went against the grain to put my watch back to midnight at 1 o'clock.

I came down to the wagon lines again today as we have had a sudden influx of subalterns; and am going off to our 'shopping centre' to buy a gramophone, 2 oil stoves etc. Such is modern war!!

I hope you are all well.

> Your loving son,
> Arthur.

10-11-17   51st Bty

My dear Mother

Just a line to let you know that I am well. Nothing new here that I can tell you; it is not so much the Bosche that we are fighting as the mud which is amazing. I don't know what to think of the general situation – who would have thought the Italians would have given in like that!

My brain is not feeling strong enough to think of anything else to say. The Major's leave is up in three or four days.

> Your loving son,
> Arthur

Passed by Censor No 3072   Field Post Office   12 Nov 1917

* * *

12th Nov   51st Bty

Dear Charles

Many thanks for your letter.

I'm at present living in a pill box, the men being in derelict tanks. When it rains the water rises & is at present 1 foot deep in here. In spite of all, I'm beginning to get quite a sentimental affection for the old place, and to look upon it as home – be it never so 'umble etc. We bail out furiously during our spare time and this morning I tried to work a system of drainage outside, but we were so continually coming upon dead Bosche in various stages of decay that we had to give it up.

I hope you have good luck in India and will be able to justify the purchase of the gun. I'm afraid I can give you no wrinkles, never having been in the

Shiny myself – though I <u>have</u> heard that it's a mistake to play poker on board ship until you quite understand the difference between a flush & a straight.

I'm afraid there is no hope of my getting leave to see you off as events are transpiring hereabouts.

There used to be a rule in India not to imbibe spirituous liquors before sundown but perhaps the march of science has done away with all that.

Well cheerio, good luck.

Your affect. brother
　　　　Arthur

*　*　*

20-1-18　　　　　　　　　　　　　　　123rd Bty　28th Bde R.F.A.　B.E.F.

My dear Mother

I've just got your letter written on the 10th. You say you received mine dated Dec 4th on that morning and I don't know whether it is you or I who have put Dec. instead of Jan.

I'm glad to hear that Biggs is keeping the available capital in circulation and hope he will make a good thing out of the willows; I'm sure there ought to be a ready sale for them when all the ammunition baskets are being made of them.

Thanks very much for writing him the cheque; I hope it came out of the estate account and not your own? I have written a 'nasty' (camouflaged) letter to Wood about finishing off the executorship accounts but have had no reply.

I'm sending on to you a slip about flax-growing which Katie sent me; apparently Staddlethorpe is to be a centre and it should be a good thing for the farmers; but as Uncle Charlie says that it takes it out of land as mustard (Biggs' bugbear) does, I don't see where it comes in just yet.

Do you see the new rates of pay? As a tax payer I must emphatically protest; I'm to get 18/- a day pay to say nothing of various allowances, which is outrageous; and as for 2/Lts getting 10/6 a day straight away, it's gross profiteering.

　　　　However, your loving son
　　　　　　　　Arthur

Passed by Censor 1563　　　　　　　　　Field Post Office 23 Jan 1918

*　*　*

15/2/18

I have the Belgian *Croix de Guerre*; I am informed by kind friends that it is a decoration *pour rire*, and the smallest of consolation prizes, – but I don't care; it's a bit of ribbon to hang on one's coat (I've a vague impression that that is a quotation from Browning) and will set off the Mons ribbon which I've just put up.

* * *

24th March 1918   British Officers' Club

My dear Mother

I arrived at the embarking place yesterday, only to find that all leave was cancelled; which was particularly annoying as I had a surprise for you in the shape of a Military Cross – *mais que voulez-vous? C'est la guerre.*

I'm afraid I was a bad prophet about the Bosche Offensives. I suppose I shall get on leave as soon as it opens again.

Your loving son
Arthur

Passed by Censor No 5802   Army Post Office 25th March 1918

* * *

4th April 1918   123rd Bty 28th Bde R.F.A.

My dear Mother

The Colonel (who was stopped from leave the same time as I was) told me today that we should both be on leave in less than a week – he expected – but he is a terrible man for passing off wild rumours for official facts, so I daresay the wish was father to the thought.

They captured a very chatty prisoner on the front who, being a schoolmaster, of course knew everything & could not tell a lie. Anyway, he asserted that no attack was impending which relieves us from the problem which has been haunting me since we came here – in the case of a Bosche advance, at what moment to order up the teams; as he would be shelling the approaches, & 6 teams of 6 horses each is a large target, one does not want them up too soon, & as I for one don't wish to be captured or lose my guns, so not too late. As they are kept some miles away, far enough to be out of the way of the usual shelling (another problem of semi-open warfare), the exact moment would be rather hard to gauge.

On the day we came down here, the horses did a 40 mile march all included, and finished up with a rather unnecessary canter into action – which was rather a shock for the poor dears after being so long in cotton wool, but it didn't do them much harm.

> Your loving son
> Arthur

Passed by Censor No 471

21st April 1918

Field Post Office 7 May 1918

123rd Bty. R.F.A. B.E.F.

My dear Mother

I was woken up last night by the Sergeant Major driving three sheep out of his room through mine to the door; he complained that they walked on his face. Later on I woke up to find a calf licking the top of my head & mooing in rather a plaintive way. I agreed with him that it was a ——— war, but asked him to go away for the present.

The unfortunate Madame returned yesterday for a visit; I'm afraid our fortifications annoyed her more than anything. However we promised to feed the dogs and she collected an old pair of breeches and two sun bonnets and toddled off very cheerily: rather an odd collection of things to walk 18 miles back to the battlefield for! I hope she wasn't a spy. She possessed a laissez-passer with a photograph in it so I suppose she was all right.

She was particularly surprised and hurt at our digging a large hole in her bedroom with a view to a future dugout. 'What on earth are you doing there?' I must say I felt rather cheap as there was not a sign of a shell in the area while she was here; but 'shooting, sleeping, eating, digging,' we are told a gunner should be doing one of the four all the time in open warfare.

> Your loving son
> Arthur

Examined by Base Censor   Passed by Censor No: 471   Franked 24th April 1918

* * *

My dear Mother

May 12th 1918

My dear Mother

We are having delightful weather and as we are also very quiet and still in the country, very different from the old Ypres sector, we are able to enjoy it. I'm so glad to hear that Katie is getting on well.

How did you get on with the Income Tax people in the end?

The division we have been with now for nearly a month, though beyond praise in action (at least the infantry), are almost too original in their methods out of the line. Four of them came into our waggon line in the middle of the night, met the veterinary officer in his pyjamas, proceeded to fire two salvoes at him with revolvers; he bolted for his tent, they followed & held up him & a very young subaltern while they went through their papers. The Vet now spends half his time on identification parades trying to spot the men.

About 4 days ago the Colonel of one of the battalions came into our lines (I was not there) and Nottingham (the Captain) took him round the lines and gave him tea; he particularly admired one of my horses; last night that horse was missing and was eventually found in this Colonel's stable. On being confronted with this damning piece of evidence, he was willing to swop another horse with it! Needless to say they are not Englishmen.

Leave seems no nearer; I have now put in over five months since the last one. I am thinking of writing to Great Horatio.

Your loving son
Arthur

*   *   *

10-6-18   123rd Bty 28th Bde R.F.A.

My dear Mother

It's quite nice to be away from it all for a bit; unfortunately it's started to hail and rain after a long spell of sunshine. We're getting quite a lot of this new complaint – dog disease, pig fever, or whatever it's called. It's rather like influenza really; I have escaped it so far.

I think you are absolutely right about Biggs' accounts. I have pored over his ledger often without being a bit the wiser. At the instigation of the Colonel I have put in a plea for special leave for urgent business affairs, representing that I am 'suffering pecuniary loss which I am ill able to afford through my continuous absence'. I don't know whether it will have the desired effect, but

93

at any rate it has reached Corps Headquarters – the latter are notoriously stingy about leave in ordinary times and dead against it now.

What an awful shock for poor Mrs Fullerton; I'm afraid he is an awful brute.

I have become a pelmanist and expect to be made a General in less than a fortnight – vide their advertisements.

Your loving son
Arthur

Passed by Censor No 1563   Field Post Office 11 Jun 18

*   *   *

15-7-18   123rd Bty R.F.A.

My dear Mother

I'm afraid my letters have not been up to the mark lately, but I've really been very busy. This is such a flat woody front that one has to walk miles to see some one particular part of this territory. I generally start in the very early morning – owing to cowardice – and get back about 3pm; it's a very healthy existence. He appears quiet here and is already harvesting the corn on his side of the line which looks to me (in all humility [sic]) that he is not going to advance here, or he would wait till it was ripe. We hear a rumour of his attacking again down South and are anxious to hear how we are doing. I suppose we shall get some of those beastly laconic messages – 'Our line now runs – X–Y–Z' leaving all the rest to one's imagination.

I picked up quite a good Bosche valise today, made of some sort of skin; just the thing to take home for leave, what a pity I shan't be able to use it for that purpose for another six months.

Your loving son
Arthur

P.S.   The cake and shirt etc. arrived today.

P.P.S.   I asked the dentist to send my account to me at once; will you please forward it on when it arrives.

Passed by Censor No 471   Field Post Office 17 Jly 1918

*   *   *

30th July 1918   123rd Bty R.A.F. B.E.F.

My dear Mother

We're still going on very much the same here; I imagine that our staff
is still busy 'guessing'. At present our attitude to things in general is that of
the Colonel who has just been here. He explained the necessity of all officers
knowing the country behind us in view of the extreme probability in the
near future etc. etc. and pointed out the probable line & date; talking about
knowing the country made him remember that he personally knows the
country in front of us very well which will now be very useful, owing to
the extreme probability in the near future etc. etc.; and began to hold forth
about transport in advance; which reminded him that we ought to take time
by the forelock & build winter standings for our wagon lines where we are
now, so as to be ready before it gets cold and wet. So you can take your choice.

I hope the 'flu is better?

Have you the addresses of Kirk, Martinson, and Taylor? I must have left
my notebook with them at home.

Thank you so much for the ear-defenders: they are a great success and I
shall always wear them.

                    Your loving son,
                    Arthur

                    *   *   *

11-11-18   123rd Bty B.E.F.

My dear Mother

We were just beginning a battle which had every sign of being rather a
sticky one, when this glorious news came in. We feel we ought to celebrate it
in some way but don't quite know how.

I suppose demobilisation will start as soon as we have got hold of their guns
etc. We are wondering whether we will move forward towards the frontier or
stay where we are. We have already received detailed instructions to 'divert
the war spirit of the men into a peaceful and industrial channel before that
lethargy sets in which so frequently follows the cessation of hostilities.' Then
there is the rather delicate question of acting rank. I see myself being super-
seded by a major from G.H.Q. or a Lt/Col. upon which I shall subside into
a humble captain again. Generally we don't know whether we are on our heads
or our heels.

What about this 'ere sale? Biggs has not vouchsafed me a word. Is it to come

3-10-18.

My dear Mother.

The Colonel is going on leave and I have to take his place till he comes back, so I shall not be able to go till then say about the 25ᵗʰ of this month. It's quite an amusing and novel experience commanding the brigade and considerably safer in action. There are still rumours of armistice etc etc flying about I hope they will make up their minds before we take the field again, as it is rather disturbing when in action but if Germany decides to fight on to the last you at any rate know where you stand. I am very busy taking over. your loving son

cont...

96

off now, or not? If not, why not etc. etc.? I'm afraid Aunt Margot will not be able to invest her money in war bonds.

I'm glad to hear that you have heard from Charley. I hope he's still all right – in fact I suppose he must be.

> Your loving son
> Arthur

P.S.   Of course we may start again next week.

Passed by Censor No 1563   Army Post Office 14 Nov 1918

* * *

20-11-18   123rd Bty R.F.A. B.E.F.

My dear Mother

We have only advanced about 20 miles since last I wrote, but are going off tomorrow to beyond Brussels. I understand that we are not to pass through the town.

It's a great pity we are not doing this in summer as it's lovely country and at present it's so foggy one can see nothing; but still 'it is good for us to be here'. I am anxious to push on quickly before the Colonel returns as I really don't think I can go on leave until we get to our final destination; after all one does not march into Germany every day in the week. The only thing is, I should like to see about these sales etc. I'm afraid we have missed our opportunity to sell the farms well. I wish Biggs would get on with it.

We had our host into dinner before leaving Renaix – he produced some excellent wine and was most interesting but I found that I had to tackle him single-handed all the evening as no one else even knew the French for 'the aunt of the gardener' or 'the pens and the ink of the pupils'; however after his enthusiastic toasts had been met with a certain amount of the phlegme Britannique, in spite of his 67 summers and almost total blindness, he gave us God Save the King (without words except for La La ti di), the Belgian national anthem and the Marseillaise without pausing to draw breath. He was himself a soldier, he said, having been band-master in the Civic Guard & after finishing up with a good tot of whisky he kept telling us that he was 'de bon coeur, moi, mais d'une disposition trop violent.' He had been in prison three times during the last four years, twice for 'official insulting' and once for giving tobacco to British prisoners. His stories of Bosche behaviour were certainly rather appalling, especially about British prisoners who, he declared, came through the town in shirts only, & had had nothing to eat for 48 hours. He had seen some of them break away from the gang to devour the cabbages at the side of the road 'like beasts'. Apart from unprintable stories, the civilians were not allowed to move about under any pretext, he had not seen his married daughter who lived 10 miles away for four years though she had 'presented him with a grandson' and it would have made no difference if she had died, he would not have been allowed to go.

* * *

Nov 23rd 1918   123 Bty. R.F.A.

My dear Mother,

I had a tremendous day yesterday in Brussels when King Albert made his official entry; we were about 16 miles out and rode in for the day. I have never seen so large and enthusiastic a crowd. About 12.30 we adjourned in search of food, to find that all the restaurants were closed. However we rushed into a very swell place where Monsieur le Patron with much gesticulation assured us that the cooks and waiters had downed tools for the day, but eventually we were informed that Madame proposed to 'faire une petite soupe' and we were invited to lunch en famille. The 'petite soupe' turned out to be a tremendous do. Monsieur, who was rather the typical restaurateur of the best type – fat, with small imperial, and bald head – would rise at intervals and remark 'Messieurs, je suis heureux de vous voir; et je voudrais que vous me donnez l'honneur de prendre un petit verre de vin avec moi'. We started with sherry, went on to some sort of white wine, claret followed with the meat, champagne & finally cognac with some 'tres bon café' & a cigar of cigars; upon which, 'mighty merry' as Mr. Pepys has it, we sallied forth with Henri and another small son to the Grande Place to see the King make his bow from the Hotel de Ville which is an extraordinarily fine building. We had to wait two hours before he appeared with the Queen & a small princess person, whereupon we all sang something about 'Le Roi, la Loi, la Liberté' & departed.

Do you remember the evening in Amsterdam when the Princess Wilhelmina was born? Well, it was the same sort of thing last night, only more so. Crowds of people in all the main squares & streets, with soldiers of all nationalities. You would meet one party dancing a sort of Scotch reel & singing God save the King, under the impression apparently that it was a kind of national 'song and dance'; then a procession of City Fathers – at least they wore top hats – would push through chanting some more about 'Le Roi, la Loi, la Liberté'; and then another lot would start rushing along,

98

shouting the Marseillaise; three elderly nuns accosted us, the eldest saying 'Americains? – Nong, Angly' whereupon they each extracted the right flag, waved it above their heads and shouted 'Ip ip Ourah' which I thought was rather a comic touch. I was with our Adjutant who is generally very much the staid old bachelor but he was quite carried away with it all, so we disported ourselves until we remembered the 16 miles of frosty road home & went off.

I hope you are all well. I'm glad to hear that the sale is proceeding. I think Biggs and the auctioneer between them should be able to give an opinion about the date, but I've no doubt it would be a good thing to point out to him about the General Election. I must say I think old Lloyd George will have it all his own way.

> Your loving son
> Arthur

Passed by Censor No 1563   Field Post Office 26 November 1918

*　　*　　*

27-11-18   123rd Bty R.F.A. B.E.F.

My dear Mother

We are still progressing slowly towards the frontier and now about 20 miles S.E. of Louvain. The Colonel has just arrived back having 'jumped lorries' from Lille about 80 miles. So I am back at the battery again. It was an interesting experience to be Brigade Commander for three weeks, especially at this time. I hope we push on quickly to our final destination which is supposed to be beyond Cologne; then I hope to get on leave and remain over Christmas. I don't think I can leave until we have crossed the Rhine.

I went to see the battlefield of Waterloo two days ago. It made me realise we were at peace again (more or less) to find a lot of greasy old men trying to sell me the book of words etc. for double its proper price. I've forgotten whether you told me you saw it or not; it is certainly interesting, especially to compare the differences of warfare now and then. I imagine when it came to the point one's feelings were just the same then as now. I wonder if after this war, the 'pomp and circumstance of glorious war' etc. legend will crop up again and people forget about the reality. Even now people are beginning to talk about their experiences as if they had rather enjoyed them.

I'm afraid Charley may have to go to Russia yet?! I have just had a letter from him but without much news.

I wonder if you got my last letter about Brussels. I left it on the table and

99

could never make certain it went by the post. I understand that the railway over the 'belt' will be through tomorrow.

Your loving son
Arthur

P.S. Thanks so much for the blades, cake and chocolate which have all rolled up.

* * *

123rd Bty R.F.A. B.E.F.
Dec 11th 1918
(Cologne)

My dear Mother

We are in the suburbs of Cologne. I went into the town yesterday afternoon, viewed the cathedral, had tea at the largest hotel where there was a band, huge crowds of well-dressed fat looking people and chocolate cakes etc. ad lib. I don't believe there is as much food shortage in Germany as there was in England. We inspected the Rhine and the Hohenzollern Bridge and then went on to the Opera, the programme of which please find enclosed. The singing and acting was certainly extraordinary good and the best seats 5/-. I really can't remember whether you have been to a German opera; it's very different in every way from any English 'show'.

Of course we go about armed with revolvers, and as we are some of the first troops to arrive, the situation undoubtedly has a certain piquancy. Yesterday they were still free but today the British Army restrictions come into force which I believe include being indoors by seven o'clock for civilians. They say the Belgians produced some of the old Bosche orders (proclamations) for Belgium, altered the signature and the date, and had them put up.

I am busy polishing up the little German I know and learning new phrases.

Biggs writes a long letter about the position arising from Oliver's death. He proposes to let his farm in small holdings at an increase of rent of £100 a year, but says that some money should be spent in repairs. I don't quite understand from him whether the sales already agreed upon are clinched yet. John Patchett is apparently grumbling about the proportion of rent of the railway flat.

Leave at present is stopped! So I don't know when I shall get home. I hope you are all well.

Your loving son
Arthur

None of the men (or myself) have received their voting forms yet; they don't care a continental but I can see some little commotion with John Bull etc. We officially march through Cologne and across the Rhine the day after tomorrow.

*　　*　　*

11-12-18   123rd Bty R.F.A. B.E.F.

Dear old Charles,

I'm so sorry to hear you are in such 'low water'. I hope things have improved a bit by now, and that you have been able to discharge your piece in anger or at any rate march through some conquered territory. Of course I only received your letter today and it would be no use to ask for you now. I've never heard of it being done directly in the case of an officer.

We are just on the outskirts of Cologne and going across the Rhine tomorrow; the attitude of the inhabitants may be described as 'conciliatory'. We were very glad to hear of the armistice as we were just going to take up a perfectly ——— position on the banks of the Scheldt in full view.

At home Biggs continues to be a treasure though he quarrels with all the farmers in turn in batches of six at a time; but old man Wood goes from bad to worse and if his clients didn't hold all the mortgages I should change lawyers.

Instructions about behaviour towards the civilians are rather amusing. (1) Not to be harsh and unfriendly of course, (2) Certainly not to be friendly – not to take their food or turn them out of their homes, that would be most un-English, but the comfort and wellbeing of the soldier comes strictly first, that goes without saying etc. etc. At first it looked as if correct deportment would not be too easy but I've now realised that one cannot help obeying at least one of them.

It must be very trying doing little or nothing in a beastly climate, though no doubt you will have got some sort of a move on now. We certainly cannot complain of inaction or lack of variety here.

Your affectionate brother,
Arthur

*　　*　　*

My dear Mother

I have just come in from an afternoon's hare driving! Unfortunately there was some difficulty about the guns so we only had two, myself and one subaltern sharing my piece, and the Sergeant Major Farrier & Quarter-Master Sergeant sharing a Bosche gun, and fifteen enthusiastic beaters. The Farrier, who had 18 years service in India, commanded the expedition and reminded me rather of Colonel Saltmarshe in his autocratic methods, but he was certainly safe which was more than could be said for the S.M.; while, when the Quarterbloke took his turn we invariably put a bank between us. However we got six hares and were very pleased with ourselves.

I am sending you a photo of the officers of the 123rd Bty. I have not got Molly's chocolate yet, and am looking forward to getting it. I see the Government is still borrowing at 5½% which arouses the indignation of the financial edition of the *Observer*: I suppose the 'mortgagees' will be wanting 5½?

I have not heard from Biggs. I suppose he will have the sales when it is most advantageous; again I say it is a pity we could not have had them last October, but I am inclined to think that it was not Wood's fault. I am expecting the latter's bill to roll up any time now and when that is paid, I shall feel that at any rate one storm has been weathered.

We do very little work these days, and the men seem more contented; at one time they seemed to have lost confidence in their officers but now that a few have been demobilised and we have done all we can to avoid any possible grounds for complaint the feeling in the Army of Occupation has improved a good deal.

I have seen a pipe which I thought should cheer Charley's declining years and shall send it to him when he arrives.

> Your loving son
> Arthur

*   *   *

22/3/19   123rd Bty R.F.A. B.E.F.

My dear Mother

I'm very glad to hear that Charley has arrived all right; I hope his temper remains normal after the Shiny.

We are to go to Aldershot after all instead of Woolwich and have begun getting rid of our horses; rather a sad occasion but I shall be glad when they 'ring down the curtain' on this act and start the next one somewhere else; this is all rather an anti-climax and I am very tired of being a sort of Captain Reece (of the Mantelpiece). Meanwhile we have been told that no more men can go on leave or be demobilised until the strikes are over, which I hope will bring the unreasonableness of the strikers home to the soldierman; but they will probably put all the blame on the government. We have not got Friday's paper yet so I don't know whether they really have struck. I have just been talking to a pessimistic gentleman who points out that there have been other civilisations in the past of which we now know nothing except by excavations and says that they were probably destroyed by Bolshevism in one form or another; and that the inevitable circle of Mankind is barbarism–feudalism–absolutism–capitalism–democracy–bolshevism–barbarism and that it may be our turn to go now. But I hope it is not quite as bad as that.

I hope you will make the motor go all right in the end.

We have got into a thoroughly peacetime way of working accounts and supplies and the amount of work which this reduction to cadre strength means to the Quartermaster sergeant, the battery clerk and me, is astounding. In wartime of course, anything 'deficient' was put down as destroyed by shell fire & anything surplus was explained as having been salved, but alas, things are not so easy now.

> Your loving son
> Arthur

P.S.   I imagine we will get home when the strikes are over.

*   *   *

March 28th   123rd Bty RFA BEF

Dear C.

I'm very glad to hear that you have arrived safely from the Shiny, and hope I shall be in England soon and see you there. I see we are to have Mesopotamia so I imagine that they will want some civil servants there.

I spent a happy day yesterday (eighth) as president of a military court (powers unlimited!) to try 13 Bosche for smuggling; it was rather amusing but unfortunately we had to let them all off, the military governor having apparently omitted to mention the fact that these goods were contraband until about a fortnight later. They had three lawyers to represent them who descanted at much length on the worldwide reputation etc. of British justice. We had various Burgomeisters and APMs in as witnesses and each fat Bosche swore that he was as innocent as a babe; they all looked rather like the cartoons of the German commercial traveller after the war.

We have sent away all our horses except six on loan, and are very busy

Oficer Commanding
123 Batt. R F A
28th Brigade A.F.A.
B.E.F.
France

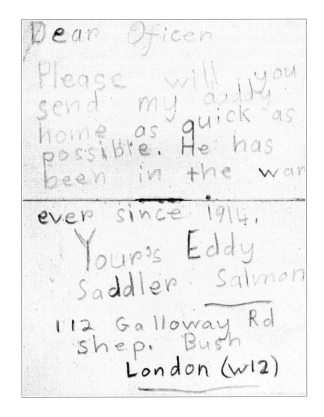

Dear Oficer

Please will you
send my daddy
home as quick as
possible. He has
been in the war

ever since 1914,

Your's Eddy
Saddler Salmon

112 Galloway Rd
shep. Bush
London (w12)

The first in, the last out.

104

reducing ourselves to cadre strength in equipment etc. which entails an amazing amount of work, and packing the stores up. I'm really very sorry to leave, I should like to have gone up the Rhine when the weather became decent. Also I fear that I shall never again get £500 a year paid regularly for my valuable services & so little to do for it.

I hope you got the motor to go!

I suppose you were too late for any hunting.

Your affectionate brother,
Arthur

Charles

1914–1918
Peshawar, Karachi,
Baghdad, Basrah

1914–1918
Charles
Peshawar, Karachi, Baghdad, Basrah

R.A. Mess
Peshawar
Friday 22nd March

My dear Mother,

My last letters from you were dated Jan 27th and arrived about three weeks ago. There seems to have been no post either way since then. I'm afraid the food question is getting bad: wish I could transport you all out here where there is plenty of everything and to spare. Can't think why they don't send food out of this country home. I suppose Arthur is a major now and will soon be a colonel. I am still stuck up here with no sign of a move and am getting more and more fed up with it. However they should send a new batch to Mesopot or Palestine pretty soon. My Cape letters certainly should have got through by Jan 27th: hope they haven't been torpedoed on the way. Am sending you another wire which should have arrived some time ago, it is going to Blacktoft as that saves five words and is almost as quick.

We had a good run on Thursday: I tried another horse. He is an awful brute for riding from covert to covert – the sort that chucks its head up and pulls and pulls – especially as it had rained hard during the night and was fearfully slippery. He did a spreadeagle once with me but did not come right over. However when we did get started he kept right in front the whole time and went some. I hoped to take both mounts out on the last day of the season – the crops are too high! – and do it in style – though a second horse is not as necessary out here as at home for we are always back to breakfast by eleven. However the meet was too far away so never got to it after all! Has Molly had a day this year? It is very odd out here, there are no games seasons as we understand them – you may play tennis, football, racquets and hockey on the same day.

The latest addition to my suite are a shikari – an awful looking villain who is occasionally entitled to wake me up at 4 am to go duck shooting (he doesn't understand a word of English) – and a munshi who is trying to drive home some Hindustani into me for one hour a day. It is pretty easy really but the alphabet is a bit of a poser.

I enclose some photos taken by a pal: the enlargements were done by a native, he is a great character and very talkative: he took us into the back of his shop yesterday and sang some Hindustani songs for our benefit accompanied by an absurd little American organ made just the size to squat down native fashion.

I am regimental officer this week and had to march church parade, there were three generals on the parade! However it passed off.

My first day's duck shooting is certainly worth writing home about. The shikari insisted that I must leave Peshawar at 4 and so I religiously arranged to be called at 3.30 and could therefore get no one to go with me. I was told how no one was allowed outside cantonments at night: all the gruesome details of the last murder: much distressing advice and many kind enquiries as to what style of floral tribute I preferred – and I had 8 miles to go. However a tonga appeared at 4 next morning all right: the wallah knew a very little English but went to the right when I told him and not left, so we set off into the night (bow-wow) and got to the Bridge of Boats over the Kabul about dawn.

Here an awful difficulty arose as the chief boatman, who with the greater part of his family waiting for us at the river, had a very great deal to say but unfortunately was unable to transfer these sentiments to me. However about half an hour later with the help of the tonga wallah I gathered he wanted Rs 10 cash down. By this time the village had come out in force to see the fun and were squatting all round smoking hookahs – and very nice and villainous they looked. I appeased the boatman in the end and he condescended to send for his boat which turned up after some time with three boatmen and we set off.

I went down stream for about 10 miles stopping at any likely places. On these occasions the shikari and one boatman and myself would land: I would walk along some distance from the bank and the boatman close to it until he saw some duck in the water ahead. He then explained whereabouts they were and with the shikari crawling behind with much excited and totally unintelligible whispering I would stalk them. This happened about half a dozen times but the duck always got up long before I was anywhere near them much to the shikari's scorn and indignation. The next place I pressed the old gun into the shikari's hands and was distinctly surprised when he proceeded to strip and do a sort of boy scout stunt along the bank: however he was no more successful, clouds of duck got up and flew back over my head but as he had the gun that was not much use.

It was now about 11.30 and all I'd got was two snipe so we landed near a village where the shikari was evidently well known and sent the boat back – the boatmen had to be called back twice, once to extract my pipe from them, and secondly a box of matches. All the village patriarchs immediately trotted out and were introduced with much salaaming and the eldest ancient lit my pipe most gracefully what time the shikari was pointing out to the boatmen the error of their ways over the matchbox. Meanwhile a brother shikari turned up and produced the secret of Kabul duck shooting. This consists of a horse hide carefully tied up and blown up with air.

Hazoor was first to have tiffin and a rest (it was fearfully hot by this time and the shikari got quite a nuisance by constantly trying to pull out my handkerchief and wipe my brow) while this gentleman shot me some duck. The shikari conducted me to an enormous three decked ferryboat worked by a man pulling at a rope stretched across and which I don't think could ever have carried a white man before judging by the excitement I aroused. On the bank a mattress and six cushions had been laid out and a blanket fixed up by way of shade but I found it too embarrassing altogether to take advantage of this for long, as they all sat around and gloated over me. I insisted on the man with the horsehide being produced, handed tobacco round, and fled. It was really awfully interesting. He would get upstream to where some duck could be seen, lie on this thing and float down onto them with an occasional flick with his legs behind him to help him on: they would let him get right up that way. I think I will try it myself one day but have only been after snipe since. I have had some very good fun.

Yesterday Haworth Booth came out too and the shikari evidently found it rather difficult to produce guns for us both. The right barrel of mine incurably went off just before I got it to my shoulder and it spouted smoke and flame from all sorts of unexpected parts of the breech. However neither of them burst and we did quite well in spite of much rain.

I was told off as range officer to a practice camp last week i.e. put out all targets, and report hits, effectives etc. – but owing to possible frontier trouble it was postponed. Please don't send my allowance out here but put it into 5% War Loan – I should lose about £10 if you sent it out. Hoping you have not been very long without a letter and love to all,

Your most affectionate son Charles.

P.S.   Have just come off a Subaltern's court martial, at which I was escort i.e. expected to put the prisoner on his back in case he had any objections. However he went peacefully and took his ten strokes of the cane very badly.

R.A. Mess
                                          Peshawar
                                    Friday 12th April

My dear Mother,

The post has come in at last – 5 weeks of it. I came to the mess for tiffin
yesterday and discovered half a dozen subalterns literally knee deep in papers
and the literature of February generally: five copies of everything from
Blackwoods to La Vie P.! I got four letters and am hastening to congratulate
Arthur: let's give the major another!

All sorts of rumours are flying about: though as a matter of fact they most
of them come from the rest of India and don't originate from Peshawar at all.
We are told that the Russians are about to pour through the pass and capture
India, that the Hun has stirred up all the border tribes, provided them with
aeroplanes and iron crosses and incited them to a pukkah show, and finally
that the 1st Peshawar Div. (poor wee us) is to go up to Landi Kotal for the
summer at the express invitation of the Amir of Afghanistan who has the wind
up – an awful prospect of heat, flies and boredom. However as Peshawar has
heard and cares for none of these things they are presumably quite untrue.
But I should like to have a go at the Russians as nothing else is being provided
for me to shoot at. (Even the snipe will be out of season in a week and I can't
get away for anything else.) The shikari tries to lure me on to all sorts of wild
expeditions but the cartridges at the club have given out and bazaar cartridges
are not only unsafe but vilely expensive. I am no nearer big game either.

The major took six of us over to the Brigade sports at Noushera (about 30
miles) yesterday – one on the step. The sports were very well done and I met
many friends – if the number of people that I asked to come up to Peshawar
and dine with me come, shall have to lead the simple life next month owing
to lack of funds. I go down to Rawalpindi on May 6th for an equitation and
rough-riding course: it lasts six weeks but of course if ordered on service will
not keep me back. Don't send any letters to Pindi though, as the course should
be over by the time this reaches you. We have to train remounts and do all
sorts of wild stunts.

It is ripping motoring here. The Grand Junction road is not at all bad and
runs practically due west from Noushera to Peshawar: there is a double avenue
of trees nearly all the way – a sort of ride on each side – and it really was quite
delightful going along about 45 straight towards the hills behind which the
sun was just setting (getting quite poetical, aren't I?). We had two punctures
though, so it wasn't all jam though it only meant a minute or two to put on
spare wheels. The second time was rather a jar though as there were no more

spare wheels and the major's chauffeur hadn't put in any patches: however after five minutes bad language we discovered it was the valve. It was quite nice to smell the native city again. By the way, old Mrs. Martin's remarks about 'liking t'smell o' Yarkfleet' would be all right to apply to a native village – you can smell Peshawar a mile away and it has quite a distinct bouquet from Noushera.

I had my last day after snipe last Sunday. We got 24 couple and a few odds and ends (you can collect a most extraordinary variety of birds here from quails to paroquets). The snipe shooting is excellent but it is a bit too late now and I missed the best part owing to lack of cartridges. The snipe from all over India get under the lee of the hills in March and April and pop over into Siberia as soon as a favourable wind comes along. I was taken out last Saturday by an old Mountain Battery major who has been here many years: he got the M.C. in Messpot and is probably the best gunner in the army and certainly the best snipe shot I've seen. I couldn't get a gun for a long time and finally managed to borrow an old duck gun from a Bombardier in the battery. We drove out about 16 miles almost to Jarkind in a tonga and found a car already at that marsh: so to a storm of oaths from the major and an old army doctor who was the third gun we set off more or less across country in our tonga to get to the next best marsh before the car could get round. We were most successful but it meant another six miles and it was 11.30 before we started. We collected half a dozen small boys from an Afridi camp close by – they are awfully intelligent kiddos with none of the cunning of the semi-civilised cantonment native and a good deal more of his sportsmanship. Now at 11.30 as you may imagine it is pretty hot and by the time we broke off for tiffin at one I was simply a large spot of lard and the old duck gun was getting heavier and heavier. Major Hunt would walk an elephant off its legs. However we had an excellent day.

By the way you say a lot about big game shooting near here in your letters but as a matter of fact there's nothing doing in that line: if I'm still here when my turn for two months summer leave comes along I'm going to have a good try and as I think I told you Haworth Booth is talking of it but we can settle nothing yet. The weather is beginning to get really hot now and we have had several down with sun: it is a most convenient way of committing suicide – take your hat off for five minutes.

Saturday
I am so sorry to see from your letters that the cables are not coming up to time. I had another post of seven letters this morning and you don't seem to have got any cables from me at all. I answered yours the same day and have

been cabling every fortnight since – lately to Blacktoft as it saves much good coin and is almost as quick. I have enquired at the Post Office though and find the cable was broken or something for about ten days so perhaps that is the reason. I do hope you are getting them all right now, though I've had no answers. Anything to Cox's is sent up here immediately – but I'm still praying to be moved soon, so please send anything to the R.A. Mess, Peshawar. We were all quite certain last month's mail had been sunk, it was a great triumph when news of the two ships arriving at Bombay came up – closely followed by the missing mails.

I hope all the epidemics have done their deedest, please don't transfer any out here as the hot weather puts enough people in hospital without these other little worries – and the last two days have been warm. However old hands say the rains have hardly ever been known to go on as long as this year, and that it will probably mean a cold summer – cold that is for Peshawar – and a famine in the Punjab. However we still keep to normal hours: when hot weather starts all work is over by eleven having started about 5, and you then get into pyjamas, or fig leaves, lie on your bed in the verandah, curse the punkah wallah, and sweat. Even now, though we haven't started punkalus yet, racquets leaves me an absolute limp rag every evening.

I enclose one or two more photos: I do wish I'd brought my camera out here but am going to get one and will send you some each week. Have not been up the Khyber yet: it is such a business getting passes and car etc. but will send you some photos of Landi Kotal before long even if the division has to go up there to frighten Russia. I don't expect you can find it on the map – just on the Afghan border in one of those independent states which are such a nuisance. The rain is keeping everything beautifully green: it is awfully pretty here, very different from barren Noushera. Still no hope of a move, two new officers arrived to the battery yesterday bringing our strength to eleven again – we sent one to Messpot the other day, and our captain went to another battery.

They seem to be having a thrilling time in France now and here I am kicking my heels about up here. Messpot is a sort of huge sports club at present and we have special chits advising officers to take out golf-clubs, guns, tennis racquets etc. as the G.O.C. is very keen on sport. Even Palestine is not particularly warlike. My only hope is the Russians through the pass: there is a major here of a mountain battery who is of Arthur's term: he has been in Peshawar since 1913 and no hope of a move yet. He and I pray together for the Russians. They'll have to hurry up though as hot weather will be too much for them too – and Peshawar always touches 125 in the shade! I have got a very good pair of glare and dust glasses to suit my eyes.

Did I tell you I had been up to Michiri and Chabkadr where the last shows were, and inspected the frontier line? It is about ten miles from here: the road runs along the frontier, there is about ten yards breadth of barbed wire entanglements and block houses every hundred yards. They used to have a live electric wire all along but were called out so many times by stray jackals and things that it was taken down. I climbed up the signal tower at Michiri and got a very good view from there.

I'm afraid that this is a dull letter but there really is not much doing at present. The normal round is parades 8.45 to 12, change into mufti, tiffin, munshi two to three, go for a ride, play tennis or racquets till 7, prop up the bar at the club (a purely social function this be it stated) till 7.45, change, dinner 8.30, bridge or anything that's going in the way of shows. It is in fact just the same as in peace time and why on earth they send people up here I cannot conceive – but then the home government are absolute lightning calculators compared to the Indian people. Just to give an example: every battery has to fire a musketry course and I have been put in charge of this: about two months ago they sent a pamphlet giving a very sensible test for each man to pass – it was all very nice and straightforward and I got about a third of the battery trained and ready to fire their course in those lines. Yesterday a chit came through to say that A.F.B. 542/N21 or whatever it is does not apply to India so we start all over again!

Believe me I am fed up. Love to all, from your most affectionate son

Charles.

*   *   *

R.A. Mess
Peshawar
2.7.17

My dear Mother,

Mails have been very wobbly lately and they have stopped publishing them in the paper so you never know when to catch them. I have been wandering about a good deal lately too.

First of all an observation course for gunner officers with the RAF at Risalpur. It was only for ten days and consisted chiefly of joyriding and picking up what information you could from the sheds but was quite a good stunt. I did a spinning nose dive and one or two other little twiddles and was surprised to find what a pleasant sensation it is: you'd think to drop down

1000 ft. would be apt to leave one's insides hopelessly behind but it doesn't a bit – you merely think what odd things the old earth is doing.

I was staying at Noushera for the course and a tender called for us every morning at 5.30. Noushera is not quite so hot as Peshawar but is rather a different sort of heat and I went down with jaundice, I believe from playing tennis before six in the evening. It caught me up in the middle of a game of footer and was distinctly unpleasant though only a very slight attack, and got me ten days sick leave. I went straight back to Peshawar – after ten days in bed – and set off with as little kit as possible and a very vague idea of where I was going. Travelled all night to Rawalpindi: got a motor there up to Murree – the cheapest hill station; it is 7500 ft. and well out of touch with railways though there is a topping road up to it through the pine woods: it turns around and back on itself in the most surprising way but gets there in the end. Murree is only open in the summer and is intended by a fatherly government to be a sort of joy city for Tommies recovering from fever and officers on leave and is always chock full. The scenery there is delightful, you look down for miles into the ravines and the air after the Plains is lovely and cool and piney but there is unfortunately nothing whatever to do. However after two days pottering around I met our captain there with his car waiting for someone to go up to Kashmir with him as the man he'd expected had failed at the last moment – so back went my bearer and most of my kit to Peshawar and off we went.

It is two hundred miles from Pindi to Srinagar the capital of Kashmir and that is the nearest railway station: every soul has to get up there by car or spend several uncomfortable days in a tonga. There are as many people and it is quite as gay as anywhere in India. There are dak-bungalows or rest houses all along the road so you can always get food and a bed: most people do the trip in about two days. Just outside Murree you switch off your engine and run downhill for twenty-nine miles – you do have to revise your idea of heights and distances here: the nearest range to Srinagar runs to 14,000 ft. and that's less than half some of the furthest ones. At Kohala you get down to the Jhelium which is just rapids all the way through the valley; only 20 or 30 yards wide it roars along as though it wants to drag you in and has cut a way down with hills practically sheer on each side. From Kohala to Srinagar you follow the valley on a most wonderful road cut into the side of the hill – at times even tunnelling through: you go up and down and twist about sometimes 500 ft. sheer drop into the river, sometimes right down close to the water. The road is jolly good most of the way but correspondingly bad in places.

We broke down just past Kohala, managed to patch her up and broke down again – this time badly about five miles further on. I spent over three hours lying on my back in the Kashmir road underneath the car, undoing the most inaccessible screws and getting thoroughly dirty. Finally some people I knew by sight came along, were very sympathetic and provided us with spare parts which after much tinkering were persuaded to work – the platinum points of our magneto had somehow been forced loose and refused to go back: my job consisted chiefly in taking the shield off the underneath of the car, grubbing about in the six inches of grease for the tiny screws Millett kept dropping down into it, and putting it on again: have since concocted a very good scheme for trapdoors in the shield, I am looking for some big company to take it up! After another hour wrestling we chased after our benefactors and actually caught them up and we turned in at the same dak bungalow.

There was a biggish storm that night and we were warned against landslides, hearing the most gruesome tales of people being carried over by falling rocks – as a matter of fact these native drivers are responsible for a good many more accidents than we hear of: they take these corners on two wheels (all blind turnings of course) lose their heads when they find themselves on top of something and may do anything. I saw a small landslide come down the next day but the road was only seriously held up in one place – it was in fact covered up all together – but coolies crop up from somewhere and clear a way in no time. We broke down again most pathetically after about five miles: and the other people who were following in case we needed help also gave way just behind and in full view. However we got her fairly started this time and eventually decided to go right on to Srinagar about 90 miles that night.

We arrived about 9 pm with no lights and as is usual in Indian places landed slap in the middle of a crowded bazaar and were soon in the centre of an admiring concourse, none of whom appeared to know their own language or anyone else's and when addressed either stared stolidly or splashed out a torrent of quite unintelligible gibberish. However we finally nosed out a big hotel quite crowded with a dance going on. I had fondly imagined Kashmir to be a simple life sort of spot where one wore shorts, a vest and no stockings and had brought no evening clothes so had to sit down to dinner in all my grease stains surrounded by hordes of boiled shirts and beauteous damsels and a horrible smell of paraffin which I poured over myself in vain endeavour to get fairly clean.

Next day we spent a happy morning taking the car down again and then set off to find our house boat – you live on house boats in Kashmir, they are of all sizes from the floating palace of the I.C.S., Maharajahs, and carpet Kings to the barge covered with matting of the impecunious subaltern, and they are as the sands on the seashore in number: there's practically not a white woman on the plains now, and hundreds of officers on leave from Messpot, Salonica and the Plains. The river is very like the Thames: it opens out into the plain of Kashmir at Barxmola about 40 miles from Srinagar – the road all that way is through an almost perfect poplar avenue like a French road – becoming quite broad almost sluggish and opening out into large lakes covered with waterlilies. As there are these snow clad hills all round and roses and all sorts of flowers grow wild and the climate is rather like a hot English summer with no bother about mosquitoes, punkahs and iced drinks you may imagine it is a pretty good spot – some blithering idiot sold the whole place for £70,000 in the darker ages. Most of the élite at that time were up at Gulmerg, a place in the hills about 25 miles from Srinagar, the last eight miles of which you ride on mountain ponies – it costs a small fortune to rent a place to pitch a tent in the season at Gulmerg.

However by this time the car had petered out altogether so Gulmerg was not for us and we took it to the only white motor agent in Srinagar – a gentleman who must be making money at a record speed, though he drinks as much of it away as possible. He is an amusing gentleman in his way and full of stories about his dealings with various rajahs and their cars. I asked him how he trained his men so well – for the average native if given a nut and bolt and told to unscrew takes a hammer and chisel and neatly divides the bolthead from the remainder of the apparatus – and if he taught them in Kashmir. He answered that his wife was teaching him Kashmir slowly but he found it rather a strain. I thought this rather odd till I saw his wife. No, she was not as black as your hat – a pure Kashmiri is practically white and very good looking – but she was unmistakable. Please do not think this gentleman typical of the pals I am making in India – he isn't.

It was at this stage that we first came into the clutches of the 'Kashmir Agency' who are quite the biggest sharks I've ever met. They propose to do everything for you: you simply go to the agency, put on your most engaging smile and say your best Hindustani equivalent of 'Ah've coom'. They supply you on the spot with:

a house boat
a canoe
a cook
a crolk [sic] boat
four different sorts of slaves
food, drink, cigars and coconuts
sheets, beds, blankets, pillows
guns, cartridges (seldom), fishing tackle
unlimited unreliable information
shikaris, munshis or a private baboo each – in fact all the necessities of life.

Your natural caution is killed to slumber, you pat yourself on the back and chortle to yourself as having found the only really obliging baboo in India. You beam upon him and even the undoubted discomfort of a donga house boat seems to melt away before him. A week passes: you hurry through Srinagar with five minutes between you and a disturbing interview with your C.O. when you do get back, in which to drop once more into the Kashmir agency and settle that account. The bill is handed to you with a bland air, every extra is neatly written down and opposite a sum equal to about half that article's value and our friend explains genially that they never hire anything in Kashmir for less than a month and if you only have it five minutes it's all the same – a month's hire. Even though this is Kashmir and not India where a baboo's person is protected by entanglements of barristers-at-law in his family and the absolute certainty of a court martial and a chat from the C.R.A. if you beat him with a riding crop, you cannot retaliate. You may take a blue pencil and cross out each item one by one but he will merely look pained, take another sheet and write it all out again remarking 'But Sir!' the baboo's war cry. There are several other little catches – most ingenious they are – and you find to your dismay it would have been cheaper to live in comfort in the gorgeous hotel and make your own shooting and fishing arrangements.

My week did not give me a chance: we rushed about in canoes seeing things and I think Kashmir would be hard to beat. We managed to sell the car to the richest man in Kashmir, who makes untold wealth in carpets – and when people do make money out here there's no mistake about it – and whose two sons I knew at Harrow. He took me to his bosom on hearing this but unfortunately considered himself grossly swindled over the car (quite wrongly as a matter of fact) and did not prove the fairy godmother that he might have been – in any case it wasn't my car! However I have heard from Millett who is still up there today and they have kissed and are friends again so when I go up to Kashmir again, which owing to very odd state of my exchequer, will be in some years time, shall hope for the best.

Of course I found it impossible to get back when my leave was up, especially as we had just managed to arrange a shooting expedition. By dint of much wiring I got three more days and went into the hills after bear. But we did no good, though got an immense amount of amusement out of it, as three days is just about time to get up the valley and back again. We stalked possible bear from 7 to 12 for two nights and 4 to 8 two mornings, but only two materialised and then no more than grunts in the distance. However it was most thrilling. The only bear I ever got within shot of nearly fell on my head off a tree: it was about twelve and pitch dark among the trees, too dark so we were going home; we lived in a tiny tent for the two nights and it was deliciously cold. I was in stalking boots of course and picking my way along the path when suddenly there was a great grunt above my head in a tree just below me and a great flop as the old bear met the ground but I couldn't see him – as I only had a hunting knife, the shikari being some yards behind with my rifle – that did not matter much. However was distinctly reminded of Mr Pinch's advice to big game shooters, 'When out to shoot him, first be quite sure you want to meet him.' I wish we had spent the whole ten days up there instead of wandering about Srinagar: however I feel I could write a four volume 'Reminiscences of Kashmir' and seem to have been scribbling away for some time.

So it's about time we went back which I eventually did in the mail motor – there is a seat every day and it takes you to Pindi on the second day. They are ripping cars – just ordinary touring six cylinder models – and take the hills and bad bits as though they never touched the road. The one I came in had done 30,000 miles of it day in and day out. All the winter there is a daily delivery and as all that road is under snow it must be a biggish job: from December to February cars can only go a short way and it's carried by coolies – heaven knows what the roads are like. Yet a letter goes for ½d to any part of India.

It must be getting near time to send drafts now and I should be off this month or August: I hope to Palestine, as people I have met on leave from Messpot say there is no more to do now there than here, without the amusements thrown in.

I am awfully bushed about Arthur's decorations: he must be having a fearful time now and I get misrubbler and misrubbler as the weeks flash by here and I remain out of it.

Should like to see the new foal: we are getting quite a stud now. We have got some nice new remounts in now: I didn't go on the rough-riding course as being a section commander the major wouldn't let me away for 6 weeks. What it is to be one of the world's workers!

From your most affectionate son, Charles.

P.S.   Have got pages more to say but will never stop at this rate. Please don't inflict it all on the whole of York.

*   *   *

UBIQUE

R.A. Mess
Peshawar
April 25th '18.

My dear Mother,

Your birthday present and a fortnight's mail reached Noushera yesterday – April 24th. Fortunately I motored in today for the Brigade sports and found them there, or should not have got them for weeks. Thank you most awfully for the cheque and happy returns: yes, I hope my 21st will be celebrated in the bosom of my family. It is most annoying about those cables and I do hope you have not been worrying at all: everything is so unsettled now. I'm afraid you must expect them when they come even though I send them off every fortnight. Posts come in absolutely any time. Hope my next batch won't have gone to Akora camp – afraid they were headed that way – as it will mean an extra week for them: but it was my own fault leaving that address on.

I am getting so settled down to the life here it is quite difficult to find anything to 'write home about'. I find nothing strange now in seeing filthy looking natives washing my dirty clothes in the river and beating them on the rocks by way of a mangle – a proceeding by the way quite unmatched for tearing off buttons and depriving the garments of their original shape; or, receiving as a perfectly legitimate excuse from gunners whose bungalows are not too clean that the 'sweeper (meter) 'asn't bin around'; or, my condition of peevish helplessness when my boy is not to be found when I want to dress for dinner; or, falling quite naturally to sleep for an hour at 3 pm daily after finishing with the munshi; or, calculating how much £.s.d. I really have got and how far it's likely to go this month and when . . . my credit will be through from Cox's; or, being surprised at the fact that two or three aged malis (gardeners), several in the prime of life, and sundry chokras (small boys) will do about as much gardening per week as Scoffus did in a day – the question, which applies to porters and bank clerks just as much as gardeners, should be looked upon from the point of view of pay – the entire garden staff get in a week about what Scoffus got in a day, so why worry? The roses here are perfectly beautiful and grow more or less wild so even if the mali does not mow the lawn by squatting down on his haunches and scratching up small handfuls of grass with a pen-knife, our gardens are still quite a credit to us and our mali. He turns slowly round on his axis until a little circle has been cleared and then moves on to another pitch: the lawn is not finished yet.

He is a kind hearted old soul however and loves me with a great love because, George being particularly fresh one morning, I pranced down a row of flowerpots and actually paid the bill of one rupee he brought me next day

121

(although the pots certainly did not belong to him) with much salaaming – it had been written out by some scoundrelly baboo in a fair round hand and spelling most vile, and had probably cost several pice. He trots up with a button hole now every morning and would be most offended if I did not wear it, and puts fresh flowers in my room daily.

My munshi took me down to his house in the city this evening: we had to walk quite a long way in streets much too narrow for a tonga but wonderfully clean: he gave us some lovely tea and fruit and introduced his pa. I wanted to go round the house and onto the roof garden but he keeps his women folk up there, and being Mohammedans they must not see anyone, so we were skilfully kept away. However he showed us round the biggest mosque – perfectly lovely stonework and the coolest building I had ever been in out here but quite spoilt by the two or three small windows which were fitted with quite the poorest sort of modern stained glass. We couldn't go up the minarets as they aren't safe.

My bearer rather distinguished himself at one of the native tarrarshes (feast days) the other day. I was just about to go to bed when he walked solemnly in accompanied by a very dapper Indian gentleman. They stood rather unsteadily in front of the writing table for a few seconds while I waited for some explanations: my bearer with a perfectly fatuous expression on his face, as of one who has achieved his greatest ambition at last. Finally, with a comprehensive sweep of the hand he indicated the other gentleman, 'My brudder,' he said and nearly collapsed under the table. It dawned upon me that they had been dining *en famille* not wisely but too well and that the rest of his numerous relations were probably waiting outside to be introduced in their turn. But at this point the reception was abruptly broken up. I have since gathered that the said brother had just completed 18 months hard, so a little celebration was perhaps excusable.

The other day the dhobie's mother died and when the remains had been decently burnt (I watched the procession leave the compound: there was no coffin, she was simply covered with a coloured cloth and carried along shoulder high followed by a dozen little girls covered with much nose-rings and jewellery throwing flowers at her, and a motley collection of mourners) the next day a tremendous tarrash started up about 6 pm in the servants' compound: they made a terrific row until the police turned up at about one o'clock. It was a tarrash well worthy of the poor old dear.

Afraid this is a fearfully rambling and unintelligible letter. Thank you again most awfully for the birthday present. Love to all, your most affectionate son, Charles.

My dear Mother,

We sail tomorrow at 9 am so of course with the usual cussedness of things will have to rush Cox's who store all our mufti as today is Sunday and they are shut.

Left Peshawar at 7.30 am Friday and arrived here this morning at 9 – having had a very dusty journey across the Sind desert: however plenty of ice, electric fans, and lemonade made life a good deal cheerier. This is quite a good time to go to Meso though of course we catch the last month of the heat and is certainly the best time to leave Peshawar as September deals out malaria all round there.

Karachi is a dead an' alive sort of hole – give me Scarborough in fact – but it is nice to see the sea again. I have bought a very nice little camera now so you can expect some thrilling snaps of war as it really is – but precious few, unless things look up a bit there. It is an awfully expensive business going to the front out here and have pretty well run through all my accounts now: however once on board you can snap your fingers at the Indian Government as you're under the good old Imperial paw then and can begin to save up for your first leave back to India. The Indian Government, which can lay hands on practically as much money as it likes, won't pay for any active service stunts: even a show purely affecting India like a local scrap on the frontier has all its bills sent home. All they can do is to cut down the unfortunate I. A. Officer's pay as much as possible while he's in India and really needs the dibs.

Will write as soon as possible. Please excuse hotel nib. With love to you all, from your most affectionate son, Charles.

*   *   *

My dear Mother,

Am now safely in Basrah waiting for orders to go up the river. We left Karachi on the twelfth on the *Haiyang*, an old Chinese coast mail boat of about 2000 tons – she had her bridge all caged in in case of attack by Chinese pirates but now does a thriving trade in a very mixed cargo including officers and sheep between Karachi and Basrah. However the last boat I rolled up in was a 20,000 tonner and it is monsoon weather now so the first two or three days out were a bit parlous: I am bound to say I attended every meal though perhaps did not entirely do justice to the cuisine especially for the first breakfast when there were only two of us. However when we arrived at the mouth of the Gulf it calmed down and I began to get very hot and sticky but fortunately we had a head wind all the way up and only had it really hot once or twice. We stopped on the way for two days to unload some cargo and our stokers went down with heat stroke so we took nine days over the trip instead of the usual five. We had fourteen officers on board and were very comfortable . . .

*   *   *

No 2 B.B. Depot
Makimah Masus, Basrah MEF
Aug. 28th '18

My dear Mother,

We are still hanging around Basrah and so far have no orders whatever but they should be through pretty soon now. They tell me the river is choked up and we shan't be able to go up to Baghdad for some days but as there are some thirty gunner officers waiting here for boats we'll be rather a crush when we do get off. There are several ways of going up the river: half by train and half by boat but I hope we won't have to change often as my kit is considerably over 80lbs, which is the regulation weight, and I will probably have to hump it myself. There is going to be some fighting in Persia this year and perhaps some skirmishing here – though at present we could walk right through the map if we could get the food up. However the old Turk has had about enough and I am taking the first chance of coming home I get.

Basrah is very peaceful and interesting in its way though hardly exciting. We are in huts – I am staying at the Carlton! – and quite comfy if very little to do. However there are two decent clubs where one can get tennis and billiards, we also get rounds of orderly officer occasionally. I have a spasm on me now. The climate here is surprisingly pleasant: we sleep out at nights but need at least one blanket and no mosquito net. At Peshawar I used to be on a Japanese straw mat with just a small towel around my middle and inside a sandfly net which is of very fine mesh and consequently very stuffy, in the middle of the bungalow drive, and perspire freely. It is quite cool here until about 7 am and then heats up very quickly to about 110° in the shade but it is a dry heat and not at all unpleasant though glare glasses are necessary.

124

We have a large electric fan in each cubicle too, and rows in the mess. There is one more heat wave to come on yet, just to ripen the dates up, and then I believe this is a delightful country. However a heat wave here means 130°!

This must have been a fearful spot in the past but now it's just like an ordinary Indian station only much cheaper. There is a regular bus and light railway service, policemen at every corner, heat stroke posts where you can get drinking water and first aid about every hundred yards along the road, in fact every luxury. All military too and so all free. But the joyriders on government petrol would make a *Daily Mail* reporter's hair curl.

We had a concert last night in the club (there are at least half a dozen cinemas in Basrah by the way) classical music but not quite good enough, though not at all bad. But I wish I had the 74th Battery troop I was president of out here. Basrah itself is like any other native bazaar and the base has been built in a big circle for two or three miles all round – you go through a palm forest for about half a mile and suddenly come to an enormous wireless station and electric power house, then more palms and a camp among the trees, then a hospital and R.E. dump and so on for miles. When you get to the river bank too it's a bit of a shock as there's bags of ships of all shapes and sizes anchored and something continually coming and going, to say nothing of dozens of little motor launches buzzing around. I have taken a good many photos but they are being developed at Peshawar and Karachi and various other places on the way so I hope to send you some soon if one doesn't come in time for this mail. I hope they'll be a success. It is difficult to get things done here and prices are wild, methods rather strange. A Persian watch maker put a new glass in for me yesterday and has successfully stopped my watch: much forcible language from me has I hope got the wheels to go round again but he is probably almost certainly seizing the opportunity to remove all the jewels.

I hope you got my wire all right: perhaps letters won't take so long up here though by the state of the river traffic I'm afraid it's unlikely.

Love to all and hoping things are looking up at home. The news is jolly good isn't it and I see you've had the best harvest for fifty years or something – but perhaps that was a little bit of romancing put in to fill up space in the *Basrah Times*.

From your most affectionate son, Charles.

* * *

My dear Mother,

Have had a day in Baghdad and go up the line tonight. I am not allowed to give my brigade number and don't yet know my battery so can't give you any address: but will let you have it as soon as possible. The general opinion out here seems to be that the war will be over by the time you get this, but I hope to kill a Turk first.

Baghdad is awfully interesting and not too hot. The bazaars are wonderful – miles and miles of arcades full of the most extraordinary people. We did not stop at Amarah at all but went straight on by river steamer to Kut-el-Amarah – two nights on board, stopped there one night in the rest camp, an awful place for dust and boredom, and then trained all one night to Baghdad in cattle trucks again. My train leaves here at 6.30 tonight but as I don't know where I'm going, can't say when I will arrive. Baghdad is crammed with officers and it's quite hard to get in at any of the hotels. I managed to grab the last seat at the Maude for tiffin.

Sorry can't write more just now as the ferryboat leaves here at three and it's nearly that now. They've got hydroplanes on the Tigris now!

From your most affectionate son, Charles

*   *   *

H.Q. 30th Brigade R.F.A.
MEF Basrah
Oct 10th '18

My dear Mother,

Turkey rumoured about to follow Bulgaria's example so let's hope I shall be on the way home by the time you get this, or at any rate to some other front; but perhaps we'll stop here and build roads and cabbage patches for the wily Arab. Anyway the excitement is intense. I got about nine letters last week – my first in Meso. – and they were very cheering. Hope Uncle Bill has recovered from his smash? But I suppose that was many moons ago.

Our Colonel and about four officers are on leave in England so we don't suppose we'll see them again as the last batch only started last week: two officers have come back to the battery now – one Oldham who was at Eton with Jack – and I am spare so am going to Head Quarters as orderly officer:

126

Here you have us
crossing the desert in
cattle trucks. It gives
you a good idea of
Meso miles & miles of
sweat all with two
rivers running thru' –
tho' as a matter of fact
the picture is taken in
the Garden of Eden. I
hope to see Babylon &
Ur of the Chaldees on
the way to the
Caspian, believe there
are some wonderful
statues there. At
present am in Baghdad
& go up to Shahsaban
tomorrow. Saw the
Golden Mosque today
– about 4 miles – four
minarets & a big dome
all gold surface but
they won't let an
infidel in at any price
& there's a 30 ft wall
all round.
Charles.

(8)

Kurna-Amara Railway.

127

Thought this one of Adam standing beneath the fatal tree would amuse you. As you see he has got into Khaki & his costume seems fairly decent at that, but when leaves turn Khaki down they fall' as a certain vulgar song has it. Mr. G. Robey I believe. Adam seems to have stood the strain pretty well anyway. We stopped for an hour and a half at the Garden of Eden Junction & I was kept awake all the time (2–3.30 a.m.) by a conscientious Arab saying his prayers on the platform . . . or he may have been singing himself to sleep. It was here too that a hurricane lamp, topee, camp bed, two tin trunks & a complete set of saddlery that was piled up in the corner of the truck fell over on top of me in a highly delightful manner owing to an energetic shunter. Charles.

(5)

Tree of Knowledge. Kurna.

128

British Residency Baghdad.

Christmas Greetings.

With Best Wishes
and Greetings.

From _Charle_

To _the William._

Mesopotamia,
Xmas. 1918.

Storks Nest,
Baghdad.

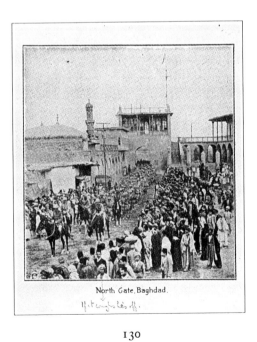

North Gate, Baghdad.

130

MOSUL
Pania
LesserZab
AltunKupri
Kirkuk
Sulaimaniyah
P
E
Shattal-Adhaim
Jabal
Hamrin
Kilri
Hamadan
Tikrit
Anah
Samarrah
Qasr-i-Shirin
Khanaqin
Diyalah
Qizil Rubat
Kirmanshah
R
S
I
KhanBaghdadi
Baqubah
Mandali
Hit
Ramadi
Fallujah
R.Euphrates
BAGHDAD
Ctesiphon
R.Tigris
Bedrah
Pusht-i-Kuh
R.Kerkha
Musaiyib
Karbala
Babylon
Hillah
Sanniyat
Kut-al-Amarah
Kut-el-Hai
Shatt-al-Hai
Najaf
Diwaniyah
Amarah
Shushtar
A
Great
Shinafiyah
Shatrah
Ahwaz
R.Karun
Syrian
Samawah
Nasiriyah
Qurnah
Suq-esh-Sheyukh
"N"
Desert
Shaibah
BASRAH
Muhamm-arah
Persian
Gulf
MESOPOTAMIA
Miles 50 40 30 20 10 0   50   100 Miles
Fao
Koweit

it doesn't mean much just now but is not at all a bad job. Anyway the old man has lent me his gun and cartridges while he's away.

We had an inspection last week by the O. C. Artillery Meso. The things I didn't know about my section weren't worth knowing. I could tell him the colour of any horse's eyes or give a resumé of its career and present prospects: to say nothing of who rode it, how many children he had, or if he was a teetotaller before he came to Meso. The great day came. We put on belts and field boots and tunics and just scintillated, a thing I haven't done for months, for don't suppose you ever wear a Sam Browne here. Normal parade costume is topee, shirt (no stars, tie or any foolish embellishments of that sort), shorts, which may be held up by anything from the best part of a Sam B. to a piece of string, cotton stockings, colour unclassified, and shoes. Our badge of rank, a walking stick. This unfortunately does not indicate the seniority of the officer: thus an object borne to be twirled in front of a band may grace a most junior subaltern, while a fellow told me he was just dashing up to tell off two strange men standing in his garden – both very disreputable but one an absolute tramp, though very appreciative of the garden, and had no stick but lovely whiskers – he was just going to let 'em have it good and proper when suddenly a very dirty (he declares they were rusty but that I hardly credit) pair of crossed swords brought him up with a click. His salute was not so graceful as usual however: the shock rather cramped his style. But when a few minutes afterwards the other tramp with no stick or shoulder straps whatever turned out to be a major-general he applied for Blighty leave on the grounds that the country was too much for his health.

However to return to our inspection. It was fearfully hot and by the time the two generals and their twelve attendants rolled up my collar had reached the unpleasant stage. They pranced up to my lines, I was introduced, 'How do you do?' 'How do you do, Sir?' then a very clammy hand to shake and then he careered round the whole shooting match at about 60 m.p.h. and never asked me a thing, though he tried to pat the only Barbary horse of the lot and would certainly have been kicked if he had been allowed to. It's a curious thing that: the higher an inspecting officer's rank the less he wants to know and the more cushy the inspection. Having been tied into knots by a mere Brigadier I expected a good deal from this man and was quite fed up to be asked nothing.

We have had no rain to speak of yet, but it has been clouded over for the last two or three days so I suppose it must come soon: I am quite dreading it after sun for so long. We had a shoot last week: I was doing range officer the first day and shooting with the battery the second – both days quite a success you'll be pleased to hear.

I hope you're getting plenty to eat at home now, we don't get any papers here at all and Reuters don't say much about the food question. I'm glad Hillas has taken the shooting again, he's a most useful person isn't he? Expect he'll keep in you rabbits all right.

Love to all,
from your most affectionate son, Charles

P.S.   Note change in address. Am now one of the world's great men – O.O. to the Colonel, i.e. general odd job man to the brigade. However it's quite a decent job as I have all the brigade staff horses to look after (30 of the best) and plenty of variety.

∗ ∗ ∗

H.Q. 30th Bde. R.F.A. 9th Nov '18

My dear Mother,

I suppose peace is being signed today but the weather is so bad I don't think we shall get the wireless through. In any case we have celebrated so many peaces in the last three weeks that they have almost ceased to amuse. The Kaiser's abdication was the first time we really blossomed out. The *pièce de résistance* was a battle royal at midnight on a small plank bridge over the canal: the water was quite cold too & a surprisingly long way down; almost everyone had a swim, some a good many. Personally I was satisfied with three: even if the old man were dead & buried nothing would have induced me to swim the Shoroban again. Being the only people with wireless we got the news first just after dinner, & soon had the Brigade going strong: Q.M. Stores were ransacked for Verey lights & a fine firework display put up, including a very sound barrage over the main road. Of course the Infantry next door thought peace was declared at last, & turned out their band which marched round the parade ground led by the Colonel beating a drum. They naturally got a bit lively & when the official denial came next morning some looked rather foolish. Since then we have celebrated many and various occasions, including two for our own private armistice when a divisional holiday gave us a pretty good show in the way of sports & concerts, not to mention the ubiquitous Verey light – it pretty well rained Verey lights that night.

Six of the 55th Bde. are staying here to play us polo and being Mess Secretary I find it rather a strain, especially as I was just dragging the mess in when they arrived & it has rained hard ever since. Most unexpected at this time of the year. This morning my forage was swimming about in two feet of water, the men's cook-house just mud with a fire in the middle, and our own

133

slowly crumbling away to the utter despair of our new cook. The mess has stood up well however, though as it never had time to dry I had to cover all the seats and tables with horse rugs & we find it impossible to get rid of a fine family of frogs. I hadn't time to get the fireplace dug out either, so we dined in British warms, which is certainly odd since last week we were living in shorts and shirt-sleeves.

November 10th

Peace came through all right yesterday & so did the rain, into our new mess: however we supplied all the visitors with spades and got it drained again in no time. A couple of inches of straw on the floor got it quite respectable again. The rain successfully stopped polo but we saw that the 55th Bde. celebrated peace night in proper style, though I had many thrilling moments when the food began to run low – 'Will it go all round?' Eleven is rather a lot to cater for. Fortunately we had plenty of beer.

We had great doings yesterday as 150 remounts came through for the Depot & we had a sort of horse fair: battery commanders exchanging their duds. I got six pretty good ones in exchange for all my worst & am hoping to get a topping little chestnut charger which is stopping here on the way from Corps H.Q.: it's going to be rather difficult to manage though.

Peace hasn't really affected us here at all, though we hope to get a move on soon. It's not really a bad country at all in its way. I would much prefer it to what I saw of India if things were civilised up a bit. I get a little shooting now & then & perhaps some fishing, but it is rather overshot just round here.

Hoping to see you again in the near future, and with best love to all,

from your most affectionate son
Charles.

P.S. Mail's very bad.

* * *

25.11.18 H.Q. 30th Bde RFA MEF

My dear Mother,

I am so sorry to hear about Cousin Katie, poor Uncle Charlie must be absolutely lost without her. We shall miss her awfully.

I hope you got my card & my last letter. Things here haven't changed much in spite of peace. We still worry along in the same old way. Hard at work getting ready for the winter just now & we can do nothing but fatigues.

Fortunately we are having a spell of lovely weather but there's an awful lot to do and our strength now is hardly up to it. However I hope for the best & a few Arab labourers to help – though all the batteries are fighting for them & one lucky me has just made a corner in the lot available. By the way you say Lord Islington is putting me up for the I.C.S.; I should much prefer a job in this country if possible & could soon pick up Arabic. I haven't done much yet as we are so far away from any reasonable beings in the native line, but should like this country in peace time. Arabic is no more difficult than Hindustani as far as I can see. They tell us there is no chance of demobilising for six months at least, but I hope to be home by then. You must have had great times when peace was declared.

I have got two little black pups reputed to be Persian greyhounds asleep on my knee: they are rather tweet but will have to alter their contours a good deal if they are ever going to look the part.

I have been doing Adjutant for the Brigade for the last few days as the pukka Adj. was away playing polo: fortunately nothing very important turned up as we hadn't a Brigade Commander either for the moment, but it's extraordinary what a lot of paper comes in. I am going out after black partridge this afternoon & hope to do better than last time which was rather a failure – we haven't got a decent dog & lose an awful lot.

How is Arthur? I haven't heard from him for ages & have lost his address. Afraid my letter writing has been a poor show lately: there's really very little to say. I hope to get leave to Baghdad for the races & think it's time we started hunting, but as far as news goes we are out of it. The weather is ripping. My mail has been doing odd things lately but I think I get most of my letters. Those addressed simply MEF get me all right or at least some of them: anything to 385 Battery is all right of course.

Love to all,
from your most affectionate son,
Charles.

Band Programme.

By kind permission of the G.O.C. Advanced Defences, the Band of the 1/98th Infantry will play the following :—

1 MARCH—" Light Cavalry "	...		Struk
2 SELECTION—" Bric-a-Brac"	...		Mongton
3 WALTZ—" Blue Eyes "	...	...	Strvus
4 TWO STEP—" Weary Willie "	...		Neat
5 SELECTION—"The Dancing Mistress "			Mongton
6 IDYLL—" Lancashire Ramble "	...		Arthur
7 INTERMEZZO—" Secrets "	...	...	Anchif
8 WALTZ—" Destiny "	...	...	Baynes
9 PIECE—" D'ye ken John Peel "	....		Douglas
10 TWO STEP—" All Aboard for Dixie "			Gibb

GOD SAVE THE KING.

Baghdad Sporting Club.

—RACES—

Autumn Meeting

□ ○ □

FIRST DAY,

Thursday, 12th December,
—1918.—

Price ′ ′ Annas 8.

3rd RACE—3 p.m.

THE KIRKUK CHASE.

Distance about 2 mile.

Rs. 200 to the winner, Rs. 75 to the 2nd and Rs. 50 to the 3rd.　A Steeplechase for horses.
Weight for class :—English and Colonials to carry 1ist 7lbs ;　Indian Country-Breds to carry 10st 7lbs ; ,
Arabs to carry 9st 7lbs.

No.	Owner	Colour, Class, Sex	Horse's Name	Weight st. lbs.	Rider
1	Capt. J. H. E. de Robeck	b.e.m.	BUCKSHEESH Blue, khaki topee.	11　4	Owner
2	Lt. R. A. G. Woodhouse	b.aus.g.	WASHINGTON Dark green, white sleeves.	11　4	Owner
3	Maj. A. H. McIlwaine	ch.w.g.	JERRY Blue, yellow sash.	11　7	
4	Mr. E. F. Wilton	b.w.g.	CHASER Red and white.	11　4	Sergt. Walker
5	Capt. G. Walker	ch.w.g.	TOMMY Blue, yellow sash, blue cap.	11　4	
6	Capt. G. Walker	b.w.g.	BILLIE Blue, red sash, blue cap.	11　1	Owner
7	Mr. R. Cadie	b.w.g.	HIGHFLYER Black, yellow hoops and cap.	11　1	Owner
8	Maj. R. J. Wilkinson	br.w.g.	CHARLIE Buff and light blue.	11　7	
9	Mr. Hosack	br.w.g.	LANCET Light blue, mauve cap.	11　0	Lt. Simmons
10	Maj. M. G. Cromie	br.aus.g.	CORNWALL Cherry and green.	11　7	Wildgoose
11	Capt. Jones	b.w.m.	JEAN Black, white sleeves and cap.	11　0	Ryan
12	Capt. R. Clark	b.w.g.	TIGER Pale green, pale blue cap.	11　7	Cpl. Gray

137

5th RACE,—4·0 p.m. *THE BAGHDAD ST. LEGER.* *Distance 1 mile.*

Rs. 200 to the winner, Rs. 75 to the 2nd and Rs. 50 to the 3rd. A Flat race for all horses.

Weight for class :—English and Colonials to carry 11st ; Indian Country-Breds to carry 10st ; Arabs to carry 9st.

No.	Owner	Colour, Class, Sex	Horse's Name	Weight st. lbs.	Rider.
1	Maj. G. Willoughby	b.w.g.	VIV Heliotrope, mauve cap.	11 0	Owner
2	Cpl. Lowther	b.w.g.	SOUTHERN CROSS White, purple cap and sash.	10 7	Spr. Read
3	Mr. F. F. Wilton	b.w.g.	THE DUMP Red and white.	10 7	Sergt. Searle
4	Capt. G. Walker	b.w.g.	BILLIE Blue, yellow sash, blue cap.	10 11	
5	Capt. G. Walker	ch.w.g.	TOMMY Blue and red, blue cap.	10 11	Owner
6	Maj. Hollwey	b.w.m.	NORAH Light blue, mauve cap	10 7	Lt. Simmons
7	Capt. A. G. Marshall	b.w.g.	PIONEER Green, orange sleeves.	11 0	Mr. E. J. Moon
8	Mr. H. F. Lucas	b.c-b.g.	PRINCE Dark blue, light blue, halved.	9 11	Mr. H. F. Lucas
9	Lt. D. Yelverton	b.c-b.m.	GRASSHOPPER Black, yellow sleeves and cap.	9 7	Owner
10	Maj. R. J. Wilkinson	b.w.g.	WALLACE Buff and light blue.	11 0	Owner
11	Maj. R. J. Wilkinson	b.w.m.	BIDDY Buff, blue hoops.	11 0	Sergt. Goodwin
12	Mr. Gunn	bl.w.g.	NIGGER White, red sash.	11 0	Sergt. Mace
13	Maj. J. H. McCudden	br.aus.g.	CORRAGALINE Red, white sleeves and collar.	11 0	
14	Lt.-Col. E. Percy-Smith	b.e.m.	AQUEDUCT Pink, black cap.	12 7	Owner
15	Capt. R. Clark	b.w.m.	AUSTRALIA JANE Pale green, pale blue cap.	11 0	
16	Capt. Rooker	b.w.g.	CARUSO Red and blue, halved, black cap.	10 11	Driver Ingram

138

Arthur

Turkey, 1920

Arthur

Turkey

1920

Feb 25th 1920   65th Bty 28th Bde R.F.A.

Constantinople Army of the Black Sea

My dear Mother

This failure of the mail to arrive is getting quite a nuisance; in some mysterious way the railway strike in Italy is supposed to have something to do with it. The letters may come either by sea all the way, or to Marseilles overland, or to somewhere in Italy. I got a letter from Miss Ibbs the other day which took only eight days! and hear that Aunt Margot is a little better.

It has been very cold here, but today it is beautifully warm. It's really a lovely place, snowy mountains in the distance, the other side of the Gulf of Ismid, and Prinhipo in the middle of the blue Bosphorus. I am going off with a party tomorrow, shooting for the weekend – nothing more exciting than duck, woodcock and pheasants, but I am looking forward to it very much.

I hope everything is going well with you and the house is looking a bit nearer.

We have just been inspected by Major-General Croker who commands the Division here and who used to live next door to our mess at Fermoy as Lt.Colonel commanding a battalion of Leicesters. He was rather a friend in those days but did not appear to recognise me now – he hadn't much chance really, and I thought it would be tactless to accost him!

Great joy in Constantinople when the Turks heard that they were to keep it. I think they would have cut up nasty in Asia Minor if they hadn't; as things are, a dreadnought or two in the Bosphorus is a very convincing argument, but if they no longer owned the Straits it would be difficult to reason with them.

Your loving son
Arthur

My dear Mother

I was awfully glad to get your letter this morning dated 12th Feb! I am pleased to hear that sales are completed; will you send on Wood's account when you get it? As a matter of fact, I believe I should pay less than £7 subscription to the Yorkshire Club when I am living abroad, but I suppose it is not worthwhile saying so the first year. What a business you must have had at Whitey's! Thanks so much for taking so much trouble about it. I suppose a lot of it will be useful to you eventually, though I'm afraid it will not mean much economy to you. Yes, I also had come to the conclusion that George Mennell was almost painfully honest, and a bit of an old stoopid. Poor old Scruton, I'm very sorry to hear he's dead.

We are having lovely weather here now; all the mud gone. Four of us went on a shooting expedition last weekend to a place called Sedanje on a lake of the same name, about five miles by ten. We arrived there about one in the morning after travelling in great style in a cattle truck with a brazier of charcoal and a primus stove on which we cooked dinner and rum punch (with three English servants & one Indian). We were met by a Franco-Greek who had gone on to arrange things; he was the sort of customer who wears mufflers round his boots instead of laces, & a kind of cap comforter round his head, occasionally shaves, & always wears a cheerful smile. He greeted us by saying that 'the mountains were swarming with wild boars and foxes' & when pressed further, that there were pheasants, partridges, hares and rabbits in plenty, and the house we were to stay at was five minutes away; so we captured two porters & shouldered the valises, guns etc. & set out. When we had wandered about the town for about 20 minutes, l'interpreter found he had lost his way, so we knocked up various Turkish houses and demanded to know the way to the 'headman's house', or whatever he is called. It was a fine looking house but built mostly of wood; when you got into the rather imposing front door you found the wagons etc. and a few hens; there you were expected to take your boots off, and the living rooms were upstairs. Our host was a tall elderly Turk of decrepid appearance and the manners of a hidalgo. We were shown into a room with wonderful carpets round the <u>wall</u>, and cushions & quilts on the floor which were very comfortable – but I was the only prudent one who put blankets between them & so avoided fleas!

We had all to turn out between 8 am. and 3 pm. to let the ladies emerge from the room. The only glimpse I caught of them was just as we were leaving and I was taking our host's photo, three veiled faces were squeezed into a very small window watching us depart. I longed to turn my camera onto them but thought that would be too great a breach of hospitality & might have had all sorts of consequences. We asked the old boy to dinner but he would not come because, (the Frenchy said) 'he eat like a savage without knife and fork', but his son who had been an officer in the Turkish army, came instead. On the whole the dinner was a success, although we had to address our remarks in French to the interpreter (who didn't speak English) & he passed them on in Turkish. They wouldn't take any payment for our lodging, but the old man expressed a desire to exchange cards, which we did.

The whole thing was worth a guinea a minute although the total bag for the two days was only six ducks, no sangliers or even lapins having turned up.

> Your loving son
> Arthur

I think the best address is as above, not mentioning Constant.

* * *

17-3-20

65th Bty R.F.A. 28th Bde.
Army of the Black Sea.

My dear Mother

We have had a little excitement here lately, patrolling the streets leading into Constantinople, and nabbing arms from any Turk carrying them. As the only people in the country who normally go about unarmed are British officers, we had quite an amusing time. They took it very meekly, even when our Harrldar major (Indian Sergeant Major) who was in charge of one post consisting of Indians, insisted on searching everybody and taking any sharp instrument such as a penknife or pair of scissors from them. Some of the other batteries marched up to the top of a hill more or less overlooking the town, and stuck their guns in a very conspicuous position. Anyway it all passed off very quietly & the net result was that we took over the war office and all government offices with the idea of being in a strong position when the peace terms are announced.

We are leaving here tomorrow and going over to the European side, about two miles out of the city, a place optimistically called 'Sweet Waters'. I am rather sorry to leave Bostanjik. It's really a riviera for beauty; we are a few hundred yards from the sea facing Princes Islands, and had just arranged to buy a sailing boat.

I'm glad to hear that Charles is going to buy a motorbike and hope the

William gets his scholarship. I must really write to him but we are so very full of our affairs just now that I never seem to get time. I am just scribbling this in my tent which explains the bad writing.

> Your loving son
> Arthur

P.S.   Carpets are both dearer and worse here than they used to be; but I think they would still be a good spec. if I could get them home cheap. Could you give me any hints on the subject – I suppose one ought to buy carpets to fit the rooms? I want some at Yokefleet very badly. Of course I shall have to take a blunderbuss to avoid being robbed.

*   *   *

> 65th Bty 28th Bde R.F.A.
> Army of the Black Sea

My dear Mother

I'm so sorry that you have not got my letters: I've written at least once a week! We are having quite a good time. I have just moved over to the European side of the water as advance party of the battery, and am busy pitching camp at a place called the 'Sweet Waters of Europe' (being translated). It is supposed to have been named so by Mahomet the Conqueror when he first came across to Europe.

We have now one brigade of artillery on each side of the Bosphorus, and are at present supposed to be cowing Constantinople. We sent one gun up to the Turkish War Office which 'came into action' at the far end of the square facing the building with a body of troops behind it, and solemnly waited there until our people had taken over the building. Now we have officers (who can speak French, as all Turkish officers are bound to do) whose job is to wander up and down the offices observing the actions of the Turks and asking questions – generally obstructing them, in fact. I was going on it, but before we were actually told to dispatch the officer, I came on here. I'm rather sorry as it would be quite interesting.

I really don't think that he can give us any trouble here; he is too much in a minority in the first place. But it would be a great mistake to take away Constantinople (where we can ginger him up).

I hope you will find a good house soon.

> Your loving son
> Arthur

*   *   *

Expeditionary Force Canteens B.E.F.   8th April

My dear Mother

Things are going very calmly round here now. We seem to be settled permanently at Sweet Waters and I have been sent back to Paolo, where I am now, to bring all the heavy baggage of the brigade along. I have loaded light railway trucks, I don't know how many tons each truck, and am going off with them tomorrow to 'Haidar Pasha' where they have to be unloaded again & put into a lighter which takes us up the Golden Horn to Sweet Waters quay which is at the far end; there it goes onto a light railway up to the camp. The whole thing will take about a week.

We were negotiating for a railway boat when we left Bostandjik but fortunately there was a matter of some fifty pounds Turkish 'between us' as Biggs would say (a Turkish pound is worth 4/9 this month) so we did not buy it, but 'salved' a small row boat, which we patched up to about a 'one man bailing power' before moving. One Captain Milton & I started to row it from the quay at Constantinople up to Sweet Waters and fortunately found some Turks in a motor boat who offered to tow us with many salaams; the current is really quite strong to row against. We were accosted in the harbour by another small boat with two men and a beautiful damsel, who pathetically implored us to stop a Turkish gent in another boat from molesting her. Milton, who is an enthusiastic Irishman, insisted on making for the Turk waving an oar in his face etc. He was both surprised & hurt & turned out eventually after much gesticulation to be a customs house official. Meanwhile the fair damsel made straight for the shore where her party hastily unloaded three or four bags & made off, so I suppose we assisted in a little smuggling.

I hope William gets his scholarship at Winchester, the family will then have been represented at most of the chief public schools! I hope you have been getting some letters from me lately.

Your loving son
Arthur

24-4-20   65th Bty 28th Bde R.F.A. Army of the Black Sea

Dear William

How is the world treating you nowadays? I hear that you are becoming quite
the pale student and are going to get a scholarship at Winchester which would
be a tremendous triumph!

We are living in tents and marquees in a place called Sweet Waters, which is
the 'Happy Hampstead' of Constantinople. It's really rather an extraordinary
city as you see such different kinds of people living together, and just now the
uniforms of most of the allies. I mean to say, if you sit in the window of a pub
– I beg your pardon, tea-shop – in one of the main streets, you will see perhaps
a Cossack officer with his very dashing get-up; a Greek guardsman who wears
more a skirt than a kilt, shoes which turn up at the end and have a large white
tassel affair at the top of the turn up, and an equally comic get-up for the upper
regions; also Turkish ladies very much veiled & Parisiennes very much the
opposite; Arabs; parsons of the Greek Church who apparently receive promotion according to the length of their beards and wear flowing black robes and an
opera hat with the brim knocked off; and all sorts of kinds of dago and niggers;
Sikhs with red in their puggrehs to show their holiness; gents with green turbans
which show that they have been to Mecca this year; and so on & so on. There
is a tremendous feeling among the Greeks & the Armenians about the mosque
of St. Sophia which is supposed to be the finest church in the world, and which
was captured by the Turks some four hundred years ago, but I don't think we
should make any effort to reconvert it, in spite of the reverend gents.

Let me have a letter to hear how you are getting on.

             Your affectionate brother
             Arthur

                    *   *   *

June 22nd   Same address

My dear Mother

I'm very glad you like the furs, but I wrote you a letter some time ago which
you don't seem to have got, full of chat and wishing you many happy returns
of the day. I bought them for you in the Stamboul bazaar and should like to
know whether Mr. Raphael Cohen did me down or not; what could you buy
them for in York? I'm afraid that does not sound quite right but it would be
interesting to know whether it would be worthwhile continuing operations

146

later on. I am writing on this paper with a pencil because we have been traipsing about after Mr. Mustapha Kemal's braves for some time.

We don't fire, in order not to hurt or irritate the local inhabitants; they don't fire because they want to make friends with us after getting a few concessions. Result is this sort of thing:

Nationalist commander writes into British ditto who occupies Ismid: 'I have orders to occupy Ismid, but not to fight the British. As a soldier you will understand that orders must be obeyed; therefore to avoid unnecessary blood-shed will you please go away with full honours of war'.

Reply: 'I have orders to hold Ismid but it would desolate me to fight the Turks with whom we are hoping to resume cordial relations. As a soldier you will understand, and that orders must be obeyed. Therefore to avoid unnecessary bloodshed, please go away.'

Result: The Turks occupy the country round Ismid in accordance with the best brigand traditions, and our forces put up barbed wire round Ismid & remain there, and a battleship eventually rolls up. Those are the general lines on which we are working round here at present. I am in charge of half the battery attached to a battalion occupying a place called Tirzla [sic], at the mouth of the Gulf of Ismid. At present we are not being attacked, being too near our base for the Nationalists to venture.

> Your loving son
> Arthur

* * *

June 26th 1920　　　　　　　65th Bty 28th Bde Army of the Black Sea

My dear Mother

I am delighted to hear that Charlie has passed his exam and William got a scholarship: the family is certainly prospering just now. I hope they keep Charlie in England for a bit. I thought that Molly's money might cause a certain amount of difference of opinion; Wood certainly put 6% as being the rate for trust money just now; she should undoubtedly have shares set apart for her which are absolutely safe. Old man Herbert and I would be responsible presumably if anything happened to it before Mr. Carr's death.

We are sitting behind a barbed wire enclosure at a place called Tuzla, the wire starting from the sea and forming a half-circle back to the sea again about 2½ miles diameter; it includes a very comfortable barracks in which are a battalion of Indian infantry and ourselves. The Goeben and two destroyers are in the harbour. They occasionally go out and raid the Nationalists who are occupying the next village down the coast about 6 miles away. I have only taken one gun out once; I fired four rounds which entirely cleared a very high hill which the infantry wished to occupy, & killed two of them! Poor blighters, they didn't have a gun at all, so it 'don't seem hardly fair'. When we arrived at the top of this hill we looked straight down into Gebze and the Nationalists were streaming out behind it, the bloated ones on mules & ponies; they spread themselves out on the low hills beyond and opened a tremendous fusillade at a range about double what a bullet will carry. Our casualties as usual, nil: theirs, about half a dozen. The trouble is that we can't get hold of them & they burn and massacre Greek villages in the interior without our being able to stop it. The refugees come here, and have cured me of my prejudice in favour of the Turk. Meanwhile we spend a lot of time on 'observation hill' in our enclosure, watching their movements.

By the way, isn't it about time Uncle C's money was paid up?

> Your loving son
> Arthur

＊　＊　＊

July 26th 1920   65th Bty 28th Bde R.F.A. Army of the Black Sea

My dear Mother

I got your letter today dated the 9th and had to get it out of pawn as there was only a 1d stamp on it. Mr. Austen Chamberlain is getting smart, isn't he? I'm so sorry to hear that Molly is still poorly and hope she will be all right for the holidays. I hope the Dinard idea comes off: of course you will probably find living expensive in France.

I have just seen a *Tatler* of June 30th giving pictures of the Christchurch (Oxford) Ball on June 21st. In one group there is either our Charles or his double, and in the list of names beneath, under his striking figure – a dash – just a little crushing! The group included Miss Lloyd George & Princess Cantacazune, the latter looking rather disreputable. Charles may be seen whispering airy nothings into the ear of Miss Mond, a semitic beauty, possibly the daughter of the wicked Sir Alfred.

The Bishop must think we are good people to do business with as we both sent him a cheque of £17 – I knew I had only promised £15. Biggs put my proper contribution at a tenner, so I thought £15 would probably be right.

We are still in Saghanli barracks and not a bandit within 20 miles of us. These Greeks are nearly as bad as the Turks when they get the upper hand but I believe not quite as bad.

148

This is really a wonderfully beautiful country. Water's our great difficulty here; it comes from natural springs on the mountain and of course caught & transmitted in pipes; it hasn't rained for a month so it's getting rather short. Please give my best love to Grannie.

Your loving son
Arthur

* * *

Sept 18th 1920   65 Battery R.F.A. Army of the Black Sea

My dear Mother

I'm so glad to hear that you have had a good time at Dinard & hope the night was fine when you came across or that you got a cabin after all. The Swiss hotel keepers must be making a lot; there must be some people with plenty of money still.

I went over the Goeben yesterday, which is in the bay here with Turkish officers in charge and a British sloop looking after them. It must have been a wonderfully fast & strongly fortified ship of its class in its time, but having only eleven inch guns, is now, I understand, hopelessly behind the times. She was struck by a mine twice and hit by shells five times, and was still able to carry on. The Turkish captain was most affable; he is very short and about as broad as he is long. When we went aboard he was very upset and doing the preliminaries to a court-martial. Apparently the night before a 'tent-on' boat was hoisted up onto the side of the ship and during the night the ropes had given way at one end, the ballast had slipped down to that end, and eventually she had sunk – (I'm afraid this is a landsman's account). At the time there was, or should have been, a lieutenant, a midshipman and a warrant officer on deck, but none of them heard or saw it. There were three successive 'watches' afterwards before anyone reported it to him; that was at 9 o'clock am. When we came in he dismissed the Court and explained his woes to us fully: apparently each successive officer of the watch said nothing about it so that he shouldn't get any share of the blame, and handed over to the next relief as if everything was O.K. When he found it out he passed it on to the next in the same way; which, with the Captain's telling all this to two perfect strangers, rather stamps the Turkish navy.

At present it looks very much as if we shall be coming home this autumn, possibly October, to refit for India; of course I could arrange to stay at home.

Your loving son
Arthur

149

Wishing you a merry Christmas

28th Brigade R.F.A.   *Sweetwaters Camp.*
Christmas 1920

Evidently Charles stayed in Turkey longer than the final letter suggests.

Charles

Baghdad and Cairo

1920–1921

Charles
Baghdad and Cairo
1920–21

c/o High Commission
Baghdad   Messpot
9.10.20

My dear Mother,

Just received a letter from Dinard dated the 1st Sept and one from Molly at Yokefleet. The mails have been stuck in the river for the last fortnight.

Supposi Coxus arrives on Monday mit lady and great are the rejoicings. The public welcome is to surpass anything of its kind ever seen in this ancient and sophisticated city: in fact we got an intimation that the town band was to play three hours of the National Anthem as His Excellency steps from the train: it was disappointing to find afterwards it was only a misprint for three bars. All the natives one asks seem to think his arrival spells the beginning of a new era in Mesopotamian history, but they will probably be as discontented as ever in another six months: however perhaps I am maligning them. Anyway I suppose this will mean a garden party which revolts me beyond words. They are making a most palatial office for the old man just opposite us, so he can rush in and ask why the ——— etc, etc, when necessary. I don't mind so long as he doesn't sit and brood over his effusions all day like A.T.W. and send them in to be cyphered at eleven pm – which meant high speed juggling with figures into the small hours. But Wilson had a trying time of it: we're just resting at present.

I hope you had a good time in Dinard though suppose that is ancient history now. We are having an extra spell of hot weather this year and it's still horribly warm, however can't last long. The bike is proving a godsend and I tootle off into the blue almost every day: so far have managed to wangle all petrol, oil etc. free from the civil garage but I'm afraid they'll soon twig it's a private bike. This morning three of us went down to a place about ten miles off where the Diyalah and the Tigris join to try for sandgrouse – but never fired a shot. However we had a pleasant run if bumpy.

The day before I was shooting close by the outer defences – there is a line of blockhouses all round the town and down the main line. I suppose I was about a mile from the blockhouse: some Indian soldiers appeared very stealthily and I concluded they were having a field day or something: they lay on their tummies and hid behind sand hummocks. However a lot of pigeons came over just then and I fired off gaily: our Indian friends immediately rushed forward all talking at once and showed me their magazines all full of perfectly good live rounds and explained how they had heard shots from their blockhouse and thought it was a Baddu attack and had stalked me for about a mile. I'm not going shooting after dark under those conditions. The stray Baddu always appears – appearances nevertheless are deceptive – such a peaceable party too: he sits down umpteen miles from anywhere with his sheep or his camels or his donkeys or his goats or just himself, and placidly surveys the infinite and is quite pleased to enter into conversation with a stray sahib however mad he may seem.

However I must be careful what I say about Arabic conversations as I failed to satisfy the examiner last week on the colloquial test. They produced a wild and woolly gent and told me to ask him why he had come to Baghdad. A wild stream of explanations followed: I managed to stem the flow after a few minutes and steered him into safer topics, but it was too late, he had me cold: I hadn't the foggiest notion why he had come to Baghdad or what it was all about anyway. Afterwards I found out he had come from Samarrah by train the day before yesterday bringing salt to cure hides to make rafts to bring melons, figs etc. from Mosul. Having got his salt here a Jew accused him of dealing in stolen goods and he came to the civil offices to see about it. However next March when they hold another I ought to walk home: but I must confess the standard is a good deal higher than I expected: I thought it was a 'How are you today? Have you any eggs? Where is the pen of my uncle's gardener?' sort of examination but it wasn't a bit.

I suppose Molly is more or less of a fixture at home just at present: she will fill in an old corner in the new house: where is that to be by the way? Has the White House been put on the market yet? I haven't got a horse yet but don't need one at the moment: that will come with the mud which will come with the rain and the cold weather. No bike will stand up on these roads when they are wet: you have the real cinema skid if you're not careful.

This is a considerable letter, shows we haven't much to do between the reigns or our various commissioners! You may get a postcard next week when we are replying to congratulatory addresses.

From your most affectionate son, Charles.

154

ACT III.

A month elapses, and now we see

THE GIRL'S HOME.

and the negotiations for the marriage. These being satisfactorily concluded the girl is taken away by the boy's relatives, leaving behind her

THE SORROWFUL GRANDFATHER.

ACT IV.

opens with

THE EXPECTANT BRIDEGROOM

and then

THE HOME-COMING OF THE BRIDE

at whose feet a sheep is killed before she is carried over the threshold in genuine mountaineering fashion. General rejoicing then sets in, and the actors let themselves go in

A KURDISH DANCE.

T.P.Bd.—1885—2-9-32.

[handwritten:] they didn't actually kill the sheep — but it had a bit of a fright

---

PROGRAMME.

IN THE MOUNTAINS

OF

KURDISTAN.

A Kurdish Drama in Four Acts.

Preceded by

A GLEE SONG

to set the right note, and then by

A PASTORAL SCENE

to confirm that note.

And now the play begins and the curtain rises on

ACT I.

A ROBBER GANG

is sharing out some recent spoils. They hear sounds, and

A PEACEFUL PARTY

arrives and are despoiled. The old man is killed and the son escapes. The new spoils are now divided, all except a pair of shoes about which the robbers have

A QUARREL

and one of them is killed. The boy who escaped has found help. The robbers, hearing their approach, clear out, leaving the two corpses.

THE RESCUE PARTY

recognize the dead robber. They clear up the mess, and the curtain drops (or should do).

ACT II.

Scene 1.

THE HALL OF THE MOUNTAIN KING

or the Amir and his Privy Councillors. The murdered man's son arrives and makes a

DEMAND FOR JUSTICE

The Amir investigates the complaint and gives orders for the

ARREST OF THE OFFENDERS.

They are brought before him, confess to the crime, and are sentenced to death.

Scene 2.

Before the sentence can be carried out

A NOBLE PERSON INTERVENES.

After some persuasion the Amir amends his judgment to a fine of 300 tomans. and, giving nature a helping hand to make good the loss of life, he orders that the dead robber's daughter shall marry the murdered man's son.

155

My dear Mother,

My mail's still not coming in, however a very chatty letter arrived yesterday from my hairdresser in Cambridge; I feel that this is the pinnacle of fame. I did, as a matter of fact, write to him coldly, to say that the cork had come out of my hair wash bottle and made a horrible mess in my box, and would he refund same: so hardly expected such an enthusiastic reply. Messpot must be in the public eye. But it was written before the coal strike, I'm afraid you are having a rotten time at home now and we sympathise very deeply: coal is £100 a ton here at the best of times so quite beyond the likes of us anyway, but then oil is an efficient substitute for everything. I hope it will all sizzle out like the railway strike did and expect by the time you get this, all will be well again – or soviets!

More domestic trouble. A Tommy appeared yesterday complaining that our cook had been very drunk the day before and had assaulted his wife and servant as they walked by the house, with a beer bottle, removed some of his wife's teeth and severely damaged the servant's jaw. The wife is a Baghdadi lady, by the way, probably Armenian. He did not want the matter to get in the courts but had two British officers as witnesses: seeing as "ow a political officer would deal with it', he would prefer us to cope with the cook in private and would send the servant along for the damages awarded if any. We first removed the cook's passport – before his suspicions were aroused – and then the fun began. In a garbled flow of Arabic, Hindustani and English he denied having anything to do with it. We said he must either go back to India paying his own passage and be handed over to the police at Bombay or pay a month's wages over to the defendant. He has now gone on strike, demands his passport back: an Indian is helpless without that as he is liable to produce it at any time, but having it can bolt with discretion, and it is highly unlikely that there will be any dinner tonight. He is an excellent cook too! But such is life.

Sunday's expedition took us down to Ctesiphon, the arch of the Chosroes, about twenty miles. We were told it was a seething hot bed of insurgents and exchanged touching farewells but as we met no less than six other cars on the way to say nothing of a shooting party I think you may take it from me that the country is more or less settled thereabouts. We got five brace but the main object of the expedition was sightseeing. The usual obliging natives met us at the arch and proceeded to sell coins, bricks etc., all purporting to be of great antiquity. I enclose a handful of coins: they were certainly picked up round here but what they are would be hard to say, mostly pebbles I should think. One or two looked as if they might have been coins. The lad who sold them to me when I asked if it was his father who had built the arch said it wasn't, but the French. But perhaps the French was only a general term for strange people. Anyway it is a most astonishing place, 100 feet high and can be seen easily for twenty miles in this flat country, and is still holding firm though half Solman Park, the village next door, is obviously built with bricks from Ctesiphon. Anyway I can now claim the distinction of having entered the hall of Darius the King and seen the wall where 'the moving finger wrote and having writ . . .' but perhaps that's the wall that's fallen down. We looked for the lion's den but couldn't find it. I will send you some photos when and if they come out. Between you and me I think Howden aerodrome is far more impressive and perhaps more interesting.

It is still very hot, but we live in hope. An awful calamity has happened: Mesopotamia is running short of cartridges! Shotgun I mean. The war is all over for the present and his Excellency is reported to be busily engaged in reducing staff and expenditure so don't be alarmed if I appear suddenly one morning.

> Love to all
> from your most affection son, Charles.

P.S. I have to wear a Sam Browne belt now and Arthur took mine to Stamboul. However I am sending him the bill!

*   *   *

November 15th 1920   Office of the High Commissioner
Baghdad,
Mesopotamia

My dear Mother,

I enclose War Loan forms duly filled in with cheque – the biggest I've signed: I hope I can cover it all right & leave a little surplus to take the strain of orders from here.

But the real object of this letter is to wish you & party a very merry Christmas & a happy & prosperous New Year: if Arthur is with you please pass on the compliments of the season. When is he coming out to Messpot? If he doesn't get a move on it will all be over – it is over now really. They are issuing Christmas cards but when I went to get some yesterday was told they might be ready in a month's time, so that was that. I suppose you will be in

CRICKET.

The Casuals' Club Ground at Alwiyah, Baghdad.

On July, 2nd, 3rd and 4th

THE CASUALS versus COMBINED SERVICES.

Teams.

The Casuals.

No.		How Out.	Bowler	Score.
1	P. V. Williams	Bowled	Adams	13
2	R. S. Sugden	caught Lees	Adams	2
3	C. C. Aston	Bowled	Adams	5
4	J. G Worth	Bowled	Adams	0
5	H. H. Wheatley	caught Hick	Martin	37
6	C. R. Chadwick	Bowled	Hayman	14
7	F. W. Marshall	not out		21
8	F. J. Ashton	stumped Blakeman	Martin	4
9	C. Empson	Bowled	Adams	21.
10	F. S. Greenhouse	not out		35
11	F. E. Stafford	Bowled	Hayman	15
12	Major J. I. Eadie	caught Blakeman	Hayman	0

Extras :   Byes 17 L.B. 10 Wides 5 No. Balls   32

TOTAL   ...   200

United Services.

1	F/Lt. Richardson	Bowled	Sugden	5
2	L.A.C. Goodsir	Bowled	Wheatley	12
3	L.A.C. Bennett	caught & B	Sugden	1
4	Lt. Hayman	caught Stafford	Wheatley	6
5	F/O. Adams	caught Chadwick	Sugden	0
6	L.A.C. Busby	not out		34
7	Sqd. Ldr. Lees (Capt.)	not out		12
8	Lt. Short......			
9	L.A.C. Hick...			
10	Col. Comdt. Brown			
11	L.A.C. Blakeman			
12	Pte. Martin.....			

Extras :   Byes, 4 L.B. 2 Wides   6

TOTAL   ...   76
for 5 Wickets.

UMPIRES : Major V. Guise and Sgt. Wilder.

SCORER : Mr. C. R. Grice.

Boobery Club Rules are being observed in this match. The hoisting of a red flag
indicates an 8 annas fine and a blue flag one rupee.

the new house now; I hope it's a success. Is it Mrs Waddington's? That was a very nice little house.

It's very pleasant here now: the rains haven't started & it's delightfully cool, though not yet cold enough for our lack of windows to be a nuisance. I have been trying to buy a pony & failed, also suitable Christmas presents & failed. However I am sending you one, 'but not this week'. We are busy looking for our Xmas turkey. Christmas throws a long shadow before it in this country – there won't be enough to go round you see, & chicken is a stringy substitute at best.

The river is rising very fast the island where we used to go to shoot is now under water. They say it means a flood year when it is so early, but I hope not, as the roads are practically impassable anyway during the rains without the river into the bargain. Our next door neighbour had just put up a jetty at great trouble & expense & it is now passed from view and become the standing joke of the neighbourhood. He should have known better as he is the Anglo Persian Oil Co.'s chief in Baghdad.

By the way the aerial mail touch on these letters is only to Basrah & it only makes four or five days difference, if they catch it. However it looks well on the outside.

Wishing you a merry Christmas & a Happy New Year with best love from your most affectionate son, Charles.

Just received your letter dated Oct 6th in which you say you have already got £60 odd War Certs. I enclose therefore a blank cheque for the remainder to make up the £380 odd.

*   *   *

GOVERNMENT   29/XI/20
OF   HC's Office
INDIA   Baghdad   Mesopotamia

My dear Mother,

I expect this will find you in Switzerland: hope you are all having a good time there. This should arrive in time to wish you all a happy and prosperous New Year and that you will catch all your trains and lose none of your luggage and never have a rough crossing.

There is considerable tension among the bureaucrats just now. Alas! they are being ruthlessly sent home plus large gratuities but nonetheless ruthlessly. My own position is none too secure. but as in an unguarded moment they

Lady Cox

Sir Percy Cox

160

The Arch of Ctesiphon.

Some Baghdadis.

161

gave me a three year contract, if they were to dispense with my services now the gratuity would have to be so enormous (being rated on the amount of contract left to go) that the finances of the new Arab cabinet would be severely strained. So up to the moment I am still cyphering, for no member of the cabinet has yet applied for me to be his secretary. I'm afraid I write too badly! The latest stunt is that one cypher officer must sleep in the office every night: however it couldn't be colder than my bedroom so, as the officer on night duty gets all day free, I don't mind at all.

Today is the coolest we've had yet. Apparently the first snows have fallen at Mosul and we are getting the wind of it.

We had an expedition to an old temple called Aqqar Quf about 16 miles away this morning. Though it hasn't got the definite outline of Ctesiphon and is apparently nothing but a great block of bricks about a hundred odd feet high, it is on the top of quite a considerable hill for these parts which adds another hundred feet or so from desert level, and to my mind is much more impressive than 'the arch of the Chosroes'. The latter being Ctesiphon, which is not as I believe I told you the place where the writing appeared on the wall but merely the winter palace of some Persian profiteers of about the 5th or 6th century A.D. Another illusion shattered! However this new place (Aqqar Quf) must surely be B.C. or I shall lose all interest in ruins. Hope to be able to give you impressions of Babylon shortly but that is sixty miles away in the middle of the disturbed area so it needs a little preparation and the scrounging of much petrol. Scrounging is still extensively practised in Mesopotamia. On the way back from A.Q. we patronised the golden mosque at Kadhimain and were suitable impressed.

With best love from your most affectionate son, Charles.

* * *

30/12/20   Office of the High Commission,
                                                    Baghdad, Messpot

My dear Mother

Received today your letter dated the 24th Nov. so posts are looking up. Perhaps when they have decided that they really want a railway and then do in fact build it up again we shall run to weekly mails. Sorry mine haven't come in regularly your end; afraid it is not always the post's fault but think usually I can blame them. They are thinking of bringing out a new issue of stamps but please don't mention it to any of our stamp collecting friends. By the way did you get the set I sent to Jackie Mickelthwait? It must be three months ago now & you haven't mentioned them: the ordinary issue as on this envelope up to the five rupee. It will be very sad if they don't arrive.

Things are looking brighter now though we have as much work as we can manage day & night. You say that the Haygate Key was in the Cypher Dept. the other day & suggest that I took his place: as a matter of fact one of the Meysey Thompsons has his job. But you insult me. G.H.Q. cyphers is mere child's play compared to our line of business. We've got all the F.O. cyphers now in use & merely from the money point of view that is rather terrific as a cypher costs about £30,000 to issue & each copy works out at two to three hundred – if a copy is not accounted for at any time the whole show is cancelled.

We had great fun this week as there was a fire in the Civil Buildings & a whole set of rooms was burnt out. In the morning we had to dig in the debris for the keys of the cypher safe which one of the inmates was looking after for the night: they took the entire morning to find. The fire was at about two in the morning & everyone in the place had his two or three hundred cartridges of various kinds to say nothing of some petrol tins that exploded very creditably. I should have slept soundly through the whole show only someone dashed into my room complete with revolver & other odds & ends saying that the alarm had been going for half an hour, guns going off etc., heavy firing for some time (there had too, the place isn't more than 200 yds from our front door) & no doubt the town had risen & we were being attacked etc. I expected to be massacred on the spot but instead we assisted the fire brigade who if they weren't all drunk, certainly appeared to be. Anyway the fire went out in time but left about a dozen unfortunates with neither house nor kit of any sort. Things do burn in Mesopotamia.

Meanwhile Christmas has passed off safely & when we have recovered from Hogmanay (Scotland is well represented) things will return to normal. The rains have come & the roof is leaking & I got ten brace of sandgrouse in about an hour and a half the other day. Otherwise we are slowly becoming more & more the Arab Government.

Hope Arthur is with you by now & that Switzerland was a success. I see that they are having 'winter sports' at home according to Reuters. We are having a sort of mud regatta, very like good old warp only rather warpier, & I am not likely to come home just yet.

Best love from your most affectionate son,
Charles.

*　　*　　*

High Commissioners Office,
Baghdad
7.2.21

My dear Mother,

Have just got a big mail from you at Mürren sent off on New Years Day: you seem to have had a tremendous time there and I am very envious. The fish knives and pictures also arrived safely this morning, but there is no sign of Molly's cigs. I admire the picture of the William skiing but certainly think it would have alarmed Granny. By the time you get this the exchange should have begun to rise but doubt if the rupee will reach 2/6d again. The HCL is getting seriouser and seriouser: last month's food for three came to over a thousand rupees. Hope you got home safely and were not snaffled by the customs.

Things look much the same this end. The arrangements of the Middle East Service are still undecided and nothing more will happen till after March and no one has been sacked lately. The second Spring Race Meeting is next week and I hope it will prove more profitable than the last one which was rather a mistake.

Nearly managed to do Babylon last week but we missed the train and played golf instead. Am hoping to go down next Sunday and will send you a brick if I manage to pinch one. Afraid it would be a bit heavy to send by post though.

Tarzan has now come to Baghdad and is shown twice nightly to enthusiastic crowds. Someone has started a bus service too but it is still in the new toy stage and chiefly used for joy-rides by the natives. Very pleasant weather, not too hot yet and the cold spell seems to be over, but the river hasn't begun to rise yet.

Where's Arthur now?

Love to all. Your most affectionate son, Charles.

*   *   *

Hotel Semiramis
Cairo
11.3.21

My dear Mother,

We never do things by halves, so have taken the entire hotel for this job and very fine it is. I am in room No. 477 but have two beds to choose from and most gorgeously furnished room. Winston is already here and so are most of the others so I suppose we shall get down to business tomorrow. I am a sort of Acting Temporary Secretary to H.E., but it only really means the old

164

H.C's Office
Baghdad.
18/2/21

My dear Mother
         I have got the job after all, so please address letters

         c/o Sir Percy Cox
                    Cairo
Please forward to Baghdad   Egypt
if not known

I'll further information.

No news at present but very busy

         Your most affectionate son,

                    Charles

job of cyphering: there are 18 of us from Messpot including Cox and Lady C (Auntie), the G.O.C. in chief, General Ironside of Archangel fame etc. We came to Egypt in the Hardinge complete with band and three pounders for salute firing, reached Suez this morning and are now trying to find our way about. I am terrified at the moment as you never know who you will run up against in the corridors. We brought two baby lions and a vulture with us (or rather, the 'Administrator Somali Coast' did. I thought at first they were pets he was too fond of to leave for a few weeks but find they are destined for the zoo). On the way down at Amarah I met one Driver who coached the William for his scholarship and wishes to be remembered to him with congrats: he is a member of the civil administration and beat me at billiards.

You and Molly ought to come out to Cairo and stop here on the sly. I'm sure there's plenty of room in this place. We'll only be here a fortnight though at the outside and I shall not relish going back to Baghdad for the hot weather.

From your most affectionate son, Charles.

* * *

Under the same management as   SEMIRAMIS - HOTEL
SHEPHEARDS HOTEL 7   CAIRO
GEZIREH PALACE   March 20th 21

My dear Mother,

We are leaving here on the 25th, waiting for the London mail of the 24th but don't expect you will have got my letter telling you I was coming to Cairo in time to catch that mail.

Did the pyramids this afternoon and I was suitably impressed. I wanted to climb up the big one (Cheops) but by the time we'd climbed about inside it and admired the Sphinx and his temple and had our fortunes told and fought various would-be guides and sich like it was time to go home. One guide guarantees to go over the top and return to you in 6½ minutes but I don't really think it could be done under seven. (It takes the ordinary mortal ½ hour). Anyway we did not put anything into the machine as it wouldn't work for us, and no one else seemed inclined to put a penny in so we missed it.

I hear Winston was very pleased with that bit. He goes out there to paint in his spare time (which I'm bound to say is not often): his 3rd or 4th A.D.C. tells me that it is an awful nuisance as Winston when expected to leave for the Pyramids at two, and all the cars, private 'tecs and escorting planes having got ready, does not appear till half past four. I hear the finished article is distinctly original but am not sufficiently such a very small lion as to be able to see the private view in his flat (£11 a day!). Mrs Winston is here and all kinds of interesting people – new ones always seem to be turning up: the hero of *The Road to Endor*, the book about two prisoners of war in Turkey who pretended to be mad, is here on his honeymoon; one of the Rothschilds and wife, a very odd looking party; the Sammuels; Col. Lawrence, the famous Arab impersonator; High Commissioners from all over the place, dozens of Major-Generals; Trenchard, the only Air Marshal, or is it Marshal of the Air; Salmond, some other air title, etc., etc.

I have lots to do and the conference so far has been a great success. I

Churchill, Gertrude Bell and Lawrence in front of the Sphinx.
Cairo Conference, 1921.

Cairo Middle East Conference, 1921.

Front row centre: Winston Churchill and Sir Percy Cox; second row: Gertrude Bell, 2nd from left, T. E. Lawrence, 6th

occasionally have to do sort of second A.D.C. to Lady Cox, which consists in taking her shopping, but generally manage to avoid it, and at first had to dine with all the lions in their special feeding cage but that was too terrifying for words and I now retire quietly to the grill room where the food is just as good and the people, if not so interesting to look at, are far more amusing – and where there is no private detective. Have also escaped dining at the Residency and am in constant dread of getting an 'invite' from the Sultan as I know one is imminent for the 'Mesopotamian Mission'. However mercifully I am not supposed to be here in a social capacity; our tame A.D.C.s lead a most harassed and unenviable existence.

The Hardinge is waiting at Suez to take us back and I don't want to go a bit: Cairo is a ripping place and quite cool. The great question at the moment is whether we have to pay for our drinks and extras in the hotel (board and lodging is the government's affair and very handsomely it will have to foot the bill as this is one of the most expensive hotels in Cairo), not that my drink bill is excessive, (No! No! shame!), but having had a cigar yesterday in a fit of bonhomie before the news about having to pay for extras was confirmed, and subsequently finding that it worked out about 1/6d an inch, I expect that the extras will be about as much as one would expect to pay for the *tout ensemble* in ordinary circumstances. Please note the French which is the prevailing language here and at which in spite of Miss Nelson I am very far from fluent. I have great difficulty with my washing: the only word to the point in my dictionary is *blanchisseuse* and as I know for a fact it is a steam laundry that can't be right: the *femme de chambre* talks about *élanze* or something. Please ask Miss Nelson if that's right next time you see her.

Anyway I am enjoying myself very much though it is by no means a picnic, and in spite of the above sarcasm re hotel bill etc. your British taxpayer has been saved many millions – we hope!

Your most affectionate son, Charles.

* * *

C/o High Commission
Baghdad
7.6.21

My dear Mother,

Nothing much of interest this week except a review for the King's birthday at which the armoured cars and the aeroplanes were the chief attraction: latter flew by in threes (thirty-three altogether) and it was very effective to see them

The accession of King Feisal.

appearing out of the blue – it's all blinking desert round here as you know. H.E. appeared in a very fine uniform, all gold braid and had an Arab escort. all the local notables had prominent seats and were suitably impressed.

I have not yet risen to the heights of an under-secretary. As things stand at present we shall be finally settled (in or out) by Aug 1st so be prepared for a wire about then. By the way if I ever do send you a wire apparently meaningless take it to the Bank, Leak & Thorpe's or any large firm where you feel sufficiently at home: it will save me about 2/6d a word so will be worth it. The last sentence sounds rather mysterious but the key is that we have several commercial codes here – probably 'A.B.C. Tel. Code': if Mr Storey keeps BENTLEY'S it's even cheaper. Getting warmer. We seem to have more and more to do daily. You see letters take so long here, nearly all important official correspondence has to be carried on by telegram and the result when Cox and our Winnie got chatty is just fearful – a leader in the *Sunday Observer* is nothing to it. And after next week we shall have two people on leave and probably no one to take their places.

I hope the H.C.L. is better at home: it gets wus and wus here: everyone is demanding a rise and you may be sure I shall be there, but don't expect anything will come of it. My clothes are getting in a bad state but think they'll just have to last until I get leave. Have just had an awful experience with the swagger Bombay tailor. I let him take my measurements coming through and thought I'd test them (in drill suitings) the other day. The result arrived last week and is quite impossible: the sleeves are at least two inches too short, either I've grown or they've messed up the figures a bit. But please don't stir up our friend Cutler again on the strength of this, or Anderson either as his coat is showing a distressing thinness about the elbows. Still I've worn it a lot and it's a year old now.

With best love, from your most affectionate son, Charles.

Postscript

Telepho▮▮▮
WEST▮▮▮ 6929.
KENSINGTON ▮▮ ▮
Telegrains:—
NATHIBMUS, SOUTHKENS, LONDON.

NBK/ML

BRITISH MUSEUM (NATURAL HISTORY),

CROMWELL ROAD,

LONDON, S.W.7.

13th February 1934.

Dear Sir,

Sir Percy Cox has forwarded on the
Wood Pigeon which you kindly obtained.   It was very
good of you to take all this trouble, and it now proves
that although the Wood Pigeon s in Iraq may be different
from those of Europe in regard to the colour of the bill,
in life, there is nothing to show they are different in
any way in the skins.

Yours faithfully,

L.B. Kinnear

Assistant Keeper of Zoology.

Charles Empson Esq.,
British Embassy,
Baghdad.

175

Cromwell Road, London, S.W.

_____ 17th March *1934.*

Sir,

I am directed by the Trustees of the British Museum to convey to you the expression of their best thanks for the Present mentioned on the other side, which you have been pleased to make to them.

I have the honour to be,

Sir,

Your obedient Servant,

C. Empson Esq.,
  British Embassy,
     Baghdad.
       Iraq.

C. Tate Regan

Director.

176

A Wood Pigeon (<u>Columba palumbus palumbus</u>).